ROBERT A. M. STERN

HOUSES

ROBERT
A. M.
STERN
HOUSES

THE MONACELLI PRESS

T

M

Robert A. M. Stern: Houses

S

First published in the United States of America in 1997 by
The Monacelli Press, Inc.
10 East 92nd Street, New York, New York 10128.

Library of Congress Cataloging-in-Publication Data
Stern, Robert A. M.
Robert A. M. Stern : houses.
p.   cm.
Includes bibliographical references.
1-885254-68-7
1. Stern, Robert A. M.—Themes, motives. 2. Architecture,
Domestic—United States—Themes, motives. I. Title.
NA737.S64A4   1997
720'.92—dc21   97-28065

Printed and bound in Italy

Designed by Pentagram

PAGES 2–3: SPRUCE LODGE

CONTENTS

ACKNOWLEDGMENTS

FOR THIS BOOK, WHICH FOCUSES ON THE DESIGN OF HOUSES, my first and enduring love as an architect, I am sincerely grateful to Gianfranco Monacelli, who for such a long time has provided unwavering support of my work. The entire staff of The Monacelli Press, particularly Andrea Monfried, Steve Sears, Julia Joern, and Mason White, skillfully oversaw every phase of production. I would like to thank Thomas Mellins, who helped to shape this book and steer it to completion. Ian Luna, Sara Moss, Beverly Johnson-Godette, and Jen Bilik provided valuable editorial assistance. I would also like to thank Michael Bierut for his elegant and lively book design, and Esther Bridavsky for carefully putting that design on paper. All of the photographers, credited in the back, deserve my special thanks; without their vision and skill, such a beautiful and insightful record of our work would not be possible.

I would like to thank all those individuals practicing architecture as Robert A. M. Stern Architects, without whom the body of work presented in this book would never have been realized. I am particularly indebted to Roger Seifter, Arthur Chabon, Randy Correll, and Armand LeGardeur, as well as Augusta Barone and John Berson, who have overseen much of the work shown on the following pages. Additionally, I would like to thank Raúl Morillas for his work on many of our residential interiors. The specific contributions of these individuals, as well as those of many others, are listed in the project credits at the end of this book. Limitations of space, but not of gratitude, prevent me from acknowledging individually every member of the "RAMSA team." The senior members of the firm are: Robert A. M. Stern, senior partner; Robert S. Buford, managing partner; Roger Seifter, Paul Whalen, Graham S. Wyatt, partners; Arthur Chabon, Randy Correll, Alexander Lamis, Armand LeGardeur, Grant Marani, Barry Rice, associate partners; Adam Anuszkiewicz, Augusta Barone, John Berson, Gary Brewer, Patricia Burns, Charlotte Frieze, John Gilmer, Preston Gumberich, Michael Jones, Daniel Lobitz, Thomas Mellins, Raúl Morillas, Geoffrey Mouen, Diane Scott, associates.

THE IMPOR- TANCE OF HOUSES

WHY BOTHER WITH THE HOUSE AS AN ARCHITECTURAL PROBLEM? For one thing the house presents a way to get back to first principles. By this I do not just mean a way to have intimate contact with a specific and idiosyncratic program, site, and family—clients who have a desire to make a special mark on a place—although such is very important. By first principles I also mean the fundamental relationships between form, context, local culture, and received tradition that give architecture its special resonance. This seems particularly relevant at a time when so much about our world seems to be in flux or outright insubstantial. The problem of the house is not so much one of shelter as of psychology. More than ever, the house is the center of family life, an island of calm in a sea of doubt.

America is the most house-proud of nations. The typical American house, no matter how modest, reveals in its architectural conventions subliminal and overt expressions of the realities and myths of our individual and collective experiences. No element or detail, not to mention larger issues that can be subsumed under the rubric of style, goes unconsidered in the way American houses are designed—and marketed. Lapped siding, for example, denotes a farmhouse, while natural shingles conjure up houses confronting a storm-tossed sea; porches and red-tile roofs suggest the haciendas of the Southwest, where Spaniards and Native Americans forged a socially uneasy but physically beguiling architectural synthesis. Virtually every aspect of the American single-family house—from the handling of the bricks or stone or stucco to the hurricane lamps in the picture windows and the decorative wagon wheel on the front lawn—defines who we are as well as who and what we would like to be. Houses contextualize us as individuals, communicating where we place ourselves in the wider culture. We raise architectural elements to mythic proportions and make their history our own. Every American house is a dream house.

While advanced technology represents an ideal to many European architects, and to some American architects and certainly to the American public at large, technology is an all too real and present social and psychological problem. The United States has had more than a century of direct experience with machines; our young country grew up with rapidly advancing technology and saw, before Europe did, its capacity for cultural and environmental destruction. As a result, Americans have traditionally refused to treat technology as an object of romance—for us it is the instrument of work, and that's it. Even as glass-and-metal towers have populated our downtowns and industrial processes raise our chickens and furrow our fields, we plot our escape from technology in almost infinite ways. Our fanatic participation in sports, our devotion to nature, and our deep sympathy for preindustrial handicrafts are powerful manifestations of our disenchantment with a society that otherwise would be trapped within the limited horizons of a purely circumstantial present. Yet none of us would give up our central heating, cars, computers, or whatever. So it is that very often the best modern American houses look very much like those of the past but function differently.

WHY HOLD ON TO THE PAST?

Because tradition is a gift, not some onerous weight. In this technological era of placelessness, perhaps our greatest challenge is to build up, not destroy, our relationship to the natural and built past. Every site is a form of historical evidence that must be honored as we construct anew. I very much agree with Frank Lloyd Wright who, despite his undeserved reputation for iconoclasm, proclaimed: "True modern architecture, like classical architecture, has no age. It is a continuation of all the architecture that has gone before, not a break with it."[1] Like Wright, I abhor the false modernism that claims new beginnings every Monday morning.

Some argue that tradition stifles creativity, but I do not believe that one must literally repeat the past in order to hold on to it. In fact, I think quite the opposite is true. Tradition liberates us from the stultifying narrow-mindedness that comes with an exclusive preoccupation with the here and now. Nonetheless many architects, especially those from Europe, are threatened by tradition. To a European architect surrounded by rich, venerated, and protected treasures of the architectural and urban past, tradition often seems a roadblock to new expression. But to me, gazing out at our largely banal landscape of commercialism, I see tradition as a form of lifeline. It's a question, I suppose, of whether the glass is half full or half empty. I look for the similarities between things across time. Architecture is an act of revitalization. Using new methodologies when appropriate, or old ones when they still apply, buildings give meaning to the present by connecting to the past.

Too many architects obsess about the differences between the past and the present, and in fact make these distinctions the principal hallmark of their work. Our century is thus the first in human history to have produced a virtually self-referential—and therefore to quite a few people culturally antagonistic and alienating—form of expression. The stylistic modernism of our century that calls for a fresh start with each new project has an easy appeal because it seems so simple: sweep the cultural closet bare, shape the building and the spaces it incorporates with free abandon, do your own thing! Though some notable individual work may come of this, the overall effect of such rampant individualism yields a chaotic landscape, a disrupted and diminished sense of place. I am not opposed to a good cultural jolt every now and again, but can it be that everything that came before is ipso facto wrong, that we need a new beginning every Monday morning? For me, architecture is a wonderful relay race with the torch of tradition passed from architect to architect. Sadly, too many architects see their pursuit as a free-for-all, a contentious argument among rival heirs, at best a dysfunctional family.

HOUSES ARE MY FIRST LOVE AND continuing preoccupation. My professional career began in 1965 with a beach house for the Wiseman family. Fresh out of architectural school, I was anxious to make a mark, realizing in my own immature way an unrealized work of 1959 by a former teacher, Robert Venturi. Venturi's project for a beach house had a special resonance for me, because it too had a strong model—that of McKim, Mead and White's Low House (1887) in Bristol, Rhode Island. This work was sadly torn down just as I was discovering it in the classes of Vincent Scully, another of the teachers who played a powerful role in my architectural youth and since. Scully, a great historian and critic, had written about the Low House in a remarkable book, *The Shingle Style,* which gave that late-nineteenth-century movement (of which the Low House was a part) its now widely accepted name.[2] The Shingle Style appealed to me as a high style practiced by top architects, but with enough of the purely local about it to make each of its monuments a celebration

Wiseman House, Montauk, New York, 1965–1967.

of the vernacular culture rather than a self-proclaiming statement of the architect's will.

For a young architect trying to see a way out of the deliberately nonspecific International Style Modernism that was the prevailing mode of the day, the Shingle Style was a compelling model. The focus on place rather than on a worldview was a major shift in orientation, a real break from the behavioral model that had been set before most architectural students of my generation. We had been trained to be heroic form-givers, makers of bold shapes that would at once express our individuality as artists and, by a nearly apocalyptic process, eliminate the work of all other architects. We were to embody in mass and space the unique "spirit of the time." Serving clients was hardly part of the agenda, nor was making buildings that reinforced a sense of place. I was trained to transcend the "trivialities of the local" and embrace an international culture with an International Style.

The Wiseman House flew in the face of the apocalyptic worldview. As such it was definitely not what beach houses designed by young architects were then supposed to be. True, it was "original," but its originality lay in its connectedness: it deliberately latched on to the high and low style of the time-honored but largely neglected Shingle Style. Moreover it was obsessively concerned with the idea of house—front and back, upstairs and down—and with what a house should look like in order to convey its psychological as well as its material functions. It was not a *prism pur,* not a boxlike construct sheathed in matched boards of bleached and thereby denatured wood set in opposition to the landscape. It was not inhabited sculpture. It was a family's shelter, with a distinct front and a back, clad in hand-split cedar shakes, deliberately chosen for their palpable texture and their conformity to the local vernacular.

While the Wiseman House grew out of a consideration of the past, its quirky site-specific composition, open plan, and off-the-shelf detailing made it unquestionably a product of its time. It was modern but not Modernist. With an overscaled aggressiveness that may not be everyone's current idea of a vernacular-inspired residence, the Wiseman House still embodied much, indeed too much, of the heroic I was hop-

*Beebe House, Montauk,
New York, 1971–1972.*

ing to avoid. It was, however, a sincere effort to get beyond the trap of decontextualized Modernism. By virtue of its combination of high ambition and vernacular contextualism, that first house helped to shatter the exclusively abstract model honored by the so-called avant-garde of the day.

Four years after the completion of the Wiseman House, Fritz and Liane Beebe gave me the opportunity to undertake a bigger project, and I am forever grateful to them for giving such an opportunity to one so young and inexperienced. Their site, located in Montauk, New York, was magnificent: six hundred feet of oceanfront atop a fifty-foot-high cliff. In response to the natural beauty of the place, I attempted to unify an existing guest house (which I extensively remodeled), a new main house at the cliff's highest point, and a new changing pavilion near the beach. While the integration of the three structures, completed in 1972, was not as thorough as I hoped it would be, I do think that my response was worthy of the landscape.

To maximize a sense of the site and to take advantage of the prevailing breezes, the main house employs a system of light and wind monitors. Sliding glass doors at the top of the monitors bring air and light into the center of the house. The resulting double-height spaces are treated as intermediate platforms between principal living spaces, which are separated one from another by short flights of stairs. The drama of this somewhat overly stagey strategy is further heightened by the insertion of a diagonally rotated square into the swelling curve of a baylike mass. Artificial lighting is located in the monitors, coves, and cabinets in order to avoid piercing the ceiling planes, an unfortunate effect of recessed downlights that creates what I call "ceiling acne," an architectural sickness of our time, which I continue to abhor.

The overall impression of distinct abstraction derives in large part from my interest in certain formal strate-

gies of Louis I. Kahn. Especially in the play of symmetry and asymmetry in the entrance elevation, however, a certain wittiness, à la Sir Edwin Lutyens, pointed to a shift in my interests. In my mind, all this was perfectly integrated. How the young delude themselves!

When, in 1973, Paul Henry Lang, a retired professor of musicology at Columbia University, and his wife, Ann, also a scholar, commissioned a house, their son, Jeremy, a former student of mine, was working in our office, which heightened the personal nature of the project. Though our practice was already a busy one, most commissions were for renovations. This wonderful opportunity to build a house from scratch fortuitously came at a time when I really began to have something to say—architecturally, that is.

Nothing if not ambitious, the Lang House represents an attempt to make connections between the average New England residence and some important moments in the history of architecture. To put it another way, the Langs had grand ideas and comparatively little money, and I was willing to overlook a few constructional niceties in favor of bold effects. In order to achieve high-style signification within the tight economic framework of a basically simple scheme, color and applied decoration were substituted for the elaborate detailing that characterizes most notable residential architecture.

The Lang House was a key early step in my architectural journey. The Langs' interest in juxtaposing historical imagery with functional planning supported my growing conviction that the conscious manipulation of iconographic references must be part of architecture—at the time, this was an idea that held very little currency in a profession still largely convinced that quirky form was what made buildings

*Lang House, Washington,
Connecticut, 1973–1974.*

Mercer House, East Hampton, New York, 1973–1975.

meaningful. Ann Lang had particularly extravagant ambitions for the house. When asked what she liked, she was very clear on what she *didn't* like: contorted cubes with ski-chalet-inspired pitched roofs. When pressed for further direction, she confessed that she'd always dreamed of being an archbishop in southern Bavaria. With that in mind, work began.

For the sake of economy, the house was configured to be not only boxlike but spare to the point of bare. The yellow exterior was not sheathed in stucco like the German Baroque prototypes it was intended to recall; instead, we used a new plastic paint that suggested stucco but unfortunately proved to be less than durable. Color alone does not an archbishop's palace make, so the box was shaped and modified: on the view side, it swells forward as Baroque chapels and palace facades sometimes do. It also takes a cue from John Plaw's bow-fronted cottage project of 1795. Pulling apart from the main body of the house to grab south light and take in particular views, the curving bay gestures to the vast landscape across a deep valley. The exuberant swelling curve of the garden facade contrasts with the screenlike entrance facade, which extends beyond the mass of the house to imply a formal arrival court, which is a bit presumptuous given the dirt road that leads up to it.

This flat-walled gesturing was very daring in the early 1970s, not only because it questioned accepted for-mal models but also because it asserted that a house needed to be more than just an expression of its own construction, that it should take on extra-architectural meanings. Daring too was playing with style as content—that is, saying that a house could make a statement about an individual family's dreams and not merely its demographic characteristics. The Lang House asked whether a "modern house" could be more than the thing itself, not just an inhabited construct but a content-laden sign. Could a cheap box in rural Connecticut also be a neo-Palladian Regency Art Deco farmhouse?

OVER THE PAST THIRTY YEARS, I have been lucky enough to build many houses comparatively near to one another along the south shore of Long Island, and my evolving search for a version of the Shingle Style appropriate and distinctive to our time has formed a basis for what is now a revived regional vernacular. My work has encompassed the abstraction of such early efforts as the Mercer House in East Hampton, which Vincent Scully was to describe correctly as an "unresolved" interpretation of Arthur Little's Shingleside (1881) in Swampscott, Massachusetts, with a "layered exterior and . . . curving glass bay, outside which the columns are . . . made to appear as if they were hanging vestigially from above like purely spatial rather than structural elements."[3] My practice has also embraced renovations of older Shingle Style houses, from which I have learned a great deal. My first such renovation began in 1968 when, for my own family's use, I restored the house that another architect, Thomas Nash, had built for his family in 1906. My contribution was a grandly intentioned, if somewhat crudely detailed, curving screened porch. Nash himself had added his Georgian-inspired work to an eighteenth-century saltbox, which he put into use as the kitchen—though architectural expression had evolved, over two hundred years a way of doing things had been honored.

Redtop, Dublin, New Hampshire, 1887; 1978.

ROBERT A. M. STERN: HOUSES

Maynard House, East Hampton, New York, 1891; 1979–1980.

Other renovations followed, including the total reconstruction of a fire-damaged carriage house that was transformed in 1976 for the Ferrin family. The dramatic reorganization of Redtop—a Dublin, New Hampshire, house designed by Peabody and Stearns in 1887—addressed a house that had already been vastly expanded and somewhat Georgianized just before World War I. Redtop was in part restored and in part reconfigured for the Catlin family in 1978. In 1979, I undertook to reshape and restore the derelict but virtually unchanged William E. Wheelock House (1891) in East Hampton, which had been designed by I. H. Green Jr. for the Maynard family; that project allowed me to acquaint myself intimately with the building techniques of early resort houses.

Through my work restoring and reconfiguring old houses came a deep appreciation of the Shingle Style's linguistic synthesis of vernacular and high Classical forms as well as its endless variety of possibilities. The Shingle Style has never bored me or the collaborators with whom I have shared this search over the years. In fact, to the contrary—the very familiarity of the language has been nothing short of liberating. Because my work grows out of familiar shapes and building techniques, I have been faced with the continued challenge to create new designs in ways that add reassurance to the other pleasures that architecture can contribute to daily life. I also like to think that the houses reaffirm the public realm as a place of shared value by adding to the sum total of the local context.

My thirty years of work on the East End of Long Island is a great source of pride to me. The Shingle Style, a virtually dead issue between 1930 and the mid-1960s, when I began to practice, is once again the dominant way of building on eastern Long Island and in similar seaside places. Once again the Shingle Style is the vernacular, with so many talented architects taking it up that I sometimes receive credit for houses I didn't design.

ONE OF THE PRINCIPAL PLEASURES of residential architecture is the close dialogue between the client and the architect, especially in the project's early stages, when the specific design is shaped at the intersection of the initial artistic vision—the concept—and particular functional requirements, not the least of which is the budget. This dialogue takes time, and the detailed design that results unquestionably adds not only value but also cost to the final product. Many people are understandably put off by this process. Some are too impatient, while others genuinely do not have the time. Many more fear their own appetites and the escalating cost of their satisfaction. To help overcome this situation, and to be able to contribute to the formation of house communities on a relatively large scale, from time to time we have worked with individual entrepreneurs, so-called merchant home-builders or developers, who undertake to market completed new houses. In this situation, the builder functions as the middleperson between the architect and a hypothetical or identified buyer. Because the developer house is usually not built on an isolated site but in a subdivision, the architect has the chance to realize a kind of coherent enclave or, if on a large enough scale, townscape.

For a long time I have been interested in the kind of community-building at which America excelled between the Civil War and World War II. I refer to such developments as Olmsted and Vaux's Riverside, Illinois, created in 1869; Tuxedo Park, New York, which Bruce Price designed in 1885 for Pierre Lorillard; the seven-house group created between 1880 and 1883 by McKim, Mead and White for the members of the Montauk Point Association on Long Island; Bronxville, New York, which Bates and How designed in 1892 for the Lawrence family; and the largely unrealized project of University Heights, renamed Como Orchards Summer Colony, which Frank Lloyd Wright designed in 1909 as a resort community for university professors and their families in western Montana's Bitter Root Valley.

In the mid-1970s, I found myself troubled by the failure of the standard high-density, high-rise housing that had purportedly been built to meet the needs of inner-city residents. I was also disappointed by

Charlotte Street, Bronx, New York.

the well-intentioned proposals of my colleagues to create culturally appropriate, high-density, low-rise housing in the limited vocabulary of orthodox Modernism, such as Marcus Garvey Village in Brooklyn. In reaction to these two models, I prepared a scheme for the redevelopment of such notoriously abandoned inner-city sites as the Brownsville section of Brooklyn and the Charlotte Street area of the South Bronx, both in New York City. The "subway suburb" I proposed in 1976 had some effect, as can be seen in the enclave of ranch-type houses that were subsequently built in the Charlotte Street neighborhood. Unfortunately, expediency and misplaced egalitarianism resulted in banal architecture and no real attempt at community building.

When it became clear that the do-good housing establishment could not accept the traditional suburban village as a viable model for redevelopment, I welcomed opportunities to try out my ideas that were being offered by the for-profit development community during the runaway real estate boom of the mid-1980s. Sadly, none of the work helped the urban poor. But despite the fact that these designs catered to the upper echelons of the middle class, the projects did confirm my conviction that far more Americans than get the chance would welcome the opportunity to live in a well-thought-out house in a coherently organized neighborhood.

Our "developer" work began in 1981 on the East End of Long Island when a risk-taking new developer, Harvey Shapiro, commissioned three individual houses for lots he had acquired in a new subdivision in East Hampton. Shapiro went on to create his own subdivision in Bridgehampton, Mecox Fields, where we

Charlotte Gardens, Bronx, New York.

planned seven houses tightly clustered around a private road. This layout had the benefit of preserving three acres of open fields, which were added to an adjoining farmland preserve. In the East Hampton development, we only were able to design houses to meet our client's view of what the market would accept, but at Mecox Fields, we were not only able to plan the site but also to design the houses, working at arm's length with the future homeowners. To create visual continuity and to keep costs under control, we distilled our usual Shingle Style work, establishing a limited vocabulary of details that enhanced constructional consistency. We hoped that our touch would be light enough to resist formulaic design, and I think it was. Like many of the "builder's cottages" that proliferated in seaside resorts toward the end of the last century—such as the Land Trust cottages built during 1887 and 1888 by E. B. Hall on Easton's Beach just outside of Newport, Rhode Island—our developer houses have adopted a simple overall mass with picturesquely arranged functional elements, like subsumed porches, and representative details, like multipaned, double-hung windows and shed-roofed dormers, to establish specificity.

Subway Suburb, 1976–1980.

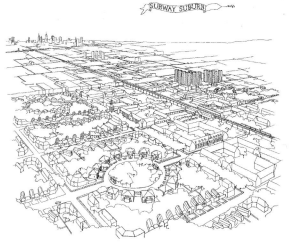

The Hamptons in Lexington, Massachusetts, is in many ways the most successful of our Shingle Style–inspired development groups to date. Six houses were grouped along a newly created cul-de-sac in one of Boston's affluent bedroom communities. The vocabulary of shingled walls and roofs, bays, turrets, and covered porches gave the group an overall coherence, but every effort was made to vary the planning and massing of each house in relation to the special features of the individual building lots. We further strove to distinguish the specific character of each house from its neighbors in order to foster the characteristics of an evolved neighborhood.

Land Trust Cottages, Easton's Beach, Middletown, Rhode Island, 1887–1888.

In 1983 we were asked to design a development, Colfax at Beden's Brook, near Princeton, New Jersey, where our plan called for twenty-three houses that would either face a common parkland or be accessible to it by pedestrian paths. Although we tried to expand our vocabulary to take into account the local vernacular, I think our houses, completed in 1987, were a bit too "Long Island." In Stamford, Connecticut, on a former estate, two of nine intended houses were completed before the collapse of the real estate market in 1988. There, however, we were more successful in picking up on the local vernacular, which not only included the Shingle Style, but also a kind of country Georgian.

At Milwin Farm, New Jersey, a small estate was transformed during 1985 and 1986 into a gated community of thirty-eight closely packed, largish houses. With no overriding local context, our primary goal was overall coherence. To meet the challenge we looked to the example set by Robert Rodes McGoodwin and other architects in their designs for house groups in Chestnut Hill, Philadelphia, in the 1910s and 1920s. Only the gatehouse and four houses were built according to our design, but the overall site plan, capitalizing on the landscape features of the farm estate, was put in place.

Milwin Farm, Ocean Township, New Jersey, 1985–1986.

Copperflagg, on Staten Island, New York, came about as the result of a special challenge posed by the New York City Landmarks Preservation Commission. The site was the estate of Ernest Flagg, a great Ecole des

Beaux-Arts–trained architect best known for designing the Singer Tower (1908) in New York City, the Corcoran Library (1897) in Washington, D.C., and the United States Naval Academy (1896–1908) in Annapolis. In 1990, Flagg erected his own Dutch Colonial–style mansion at the edge of what was once a large country property on the highest point of Staten Island. In semiretirement after about 1915, Flagg became interested in the problems of the small house and surrounded his own residence with a number of prototypes intended as exemplars of a standardized system of construction that would become a model for future developers on his property. In 1922 he published a book, *Small Houses: Their Economical Design and Construction,* which illustrated the houses and discussed the principles behind their design.[4] Flagg lived to be ninety years old, by which time he had sold off a considerable amount of his land. In his last years, when the United Nations was seeking a site for its headquarters in New York, he offered the remainder of his property.

Flagg died in 1947, but it was not until twenty years later that his house, Flagg Court, was designated a New York City landmark. In 1983, the landmark site, owned by a religious order, was expanded to encompass more of the surrounding property. The order was anxious to develop as much as possible of the property, but the Landmarks Preservation Commission was concerned that new construction would distract from Flagg's house. Our client, Sanford Nalitt, bought the land and worked with us to develop two phases: houses built on former gardens of the mansion, where the issues of contextualism were especially critical; and houses built in more outlying areas, where issues of scale and character, but not stylistic contextualism, were to govern the design. Our strategy for the garden sites was to interweave among existing Flagg-designed French Norman outbuildings our new houses, in the spirit of Flagg's designs yet with their own distinct character. A formal garden located in the basin of an abandoned swimming pool formed a community focus. On the remainder of the site, in areas that fall

Copperflagg, Staten Island, New York, 1983–1987.

Woodlynne, Bingham Farms, Michigan, 1989–1991.

outside visual corridors established to preserve the integrity of Flagg's house, prospective owners were encouraged to build unique houses under stylistic guidelines developed to stimulate variety yet maintain a compatible scale. In addition to the garden houses designed as a coherent village, we also designed five other residences on the property.

A few other house "developments" are worth noting. One, Woodlynne, undertaken by David Jensen, consisted of a twenty-four-acre portion of a former estate in Bingham Farms, outside Detroit. Two of our designs were built. The first, constructed as a model house, had brick walls and a low-pitched, hipped, shingled roof with broad overhangs, reflecting a characteristic Midwestern vernacular. This silhouette has its origins in the early work of Frank Lloyd Wright, such as the Winslow House (1894) in River Forest, Illinois. (The other house, the Gables, is discussed on pages 574–583.) In a nearby parklike setting,

Grand Harbor, Vero Beach, Florida, 1986–1989.

we designed for the same developer a red-brick Georgian-style house set between mature trees at the entrance and a steep slope at the rear. Here, interpreting the prospective owner's request for a formal, brick house, we took the opportunity to learn from the Georgian Classicism of the Tidewater region of Virginia.

Set on the Indian River in Vero Beach, Florida, Grand Harbor was to be a large resort community built around two golf courses and a marina. We were given responsibility for the design of the unrealized Harbor Center and a

separate complex, Wood Duck Island, where three clubhouses, one each for golf, tennis, and swimming, were planned. In the end, however, only sixty-seven townhouses were built. To create intimacy in a large development, we adopted a courtyard scheme. Based on the organization of Andalusian farmhouses, four standard unit types were carefully composed to frame the courtyards, while streets, paths, landscaped walls, and back gardens established a hierarchy of places so that the entire development took on not only the appearance but also some of the spatial characteristics of a village.

Two last houses, while not strictly merchant houses, belong to this discussion. Commissioned by leading magazines, both were undertaken to inform readers about new ideas in residential architecture. In 1985 we were jointly commissioned by *Builder* and *Home* magazines and the National Council of the Housing Industry to design an example of the improvements that could be realized within the confines of a typical middle-class house in a typical middle-class subdivision.

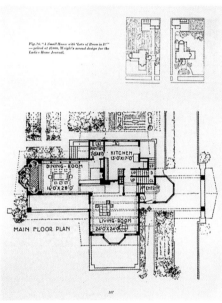

Frank Lloyd Wright house design for Ladies' Home Journal, *1901.*

Before World War II, magazines aimed at broad audiences abounded in model-house plans by first-rate architects. For example, there were two separate Frank Lloyd Wright–designed houses of 1901 for *Ladies' Home Journal. House and Garden* published wonderful annual issues devoted to house plans. But in the postwar era, this tradition died out, perhaps because top architects had one idea about residential architecture—flat-roofed and confrontational (the kind of house one's shrink lived in)—and the public had another—pitched roof and sheltering (like grandma lived in). Hand in hand with the death of the magazine house was something more serious: thoughtful architects ceased to concern themselves with the "problem" of the average family house. The absence of high-art models left the field of "home-building" wide open to the merchant builders–as–bankers. As a consequence, the American public was forced to pay good money for products it did not admire. Today, most families buy the houses they hate the least.

New American Home, Dallas, Texas, 1985.

The New American Home was built outside Dallas, Texas, so we took the simplified Texas classicism of the vernacular farmhouse as our stylistic jumping-off point. Not wishing merely to restyle the ubiquitous monster box of the 1980s, with its ill-defined sprawl of interior "spaces," we broke the house up into an assembly of distinct, symmetrical volumes scaled to specific rooms, forming a picturesque, villagelike effect. The plan was nonetheless clear, with a strong axis running from front to back like that of the Mill Neck Residence, and with pavilionated rooms opening off the axis to maximize natural light and form garden courts.

In 1994 the editors of *Life* magazine asked me to design a "Dream House," the first in a projected annual series. I was delighted with the prospect, and not only because of *Life*'s prestige and longtime influence. Many years had passed since the New American Home project, and with both the experience of designing my own house and our work on the new Disney town of Celebration, Florida, I thought a real contribution could be made. *Life* was prepared to publish but not to build the house, but within a year Stephen Macauley had commissioned a version that in 1996 was built as a show house in his Legacy Park development in Kennisaw, a suburb of Atlanta. Even without a built example, well over a thousand people bought full sets of the working drawings we prepared for the house, so there are more than likely many versions to be found around the country. We know of a few: one in Wickford Point, Rhode Island; another in Mahopac, New York; and one that *Life* featured, in Marine on Saint Croix, Minnesota.

ARCHITECTURE SHOULD BE AN affirmation of place—that is, the physical product of a truly environmentally responsive approach. The widespread acceptance in local communities of fresh versions of time-honored styles is gratifying. To work with the place and its traditions is not to be trapped in a dull set of conventions. The tension between timeless ways and the all-too-timely circumstances that call a new building into being should lead to a vital architecture. The tension between the past and the presence of the past should foster an architecture more culturally resonant than one that is either all about the past or all about the present.

One further word in response to the "why houses?" question: the house is not a mini-version of something else; it is its own distinct type. Yet the design of houses offers important lessons for architects as they move on to larger things. Large problems should not be tackled without a sense of the small. Part of the problem with contemporary large-scale architecture is that too many architects entrusted with big projects have never designed houses. They presume to know how eight hundred people can work together in an office, or how thousands gather in a public plaza, without understanding how one person operates in his or her room, how the family creates a community, or how the street, the front lawn, the house, and the backyard each support the others socially, spatially, and culturally. Without the intimate experience and understanding that comes from addressing the resonating complexities of one small building on a street in a town, how can an architect set out to help shape the larger world?

Life *magazine "Dream House," Kennisaw, Georgia, 1996.*

1. Frank Lloyd Wright, quoted in "A New Debate in Old Venice," *New York Times Magazine,* March 21, 1954, 8. Also quoted in Neil Levine, *The Architecture of Frank Lloyd Wright* (Princeton, N.J.: Princeton University Press, 1996), 380.
2. Vincent Scully, *The Shingle Style and the Stick Style* (New Haven, Conn.: Yale University Press, 1955).
3. Vincent Scully, *The Shingle Style Today, or the Historian's Revenge* (New York: George Braziller, 1974), 33.
4. Ernest Flagg, *Small Houses: Their Economical Design and Construction* (New York: Charles Scribner's Sons, 1922).

WESTCHESTER COUNTY RESIDENCE

WESTCHESTER COUNTY, NEW YORK 1974–1976

Exploring some of the ideas of the Lang House, but with finer materials and less explicit imagery, this house was, in its way, a grand Modern country house. Spaces of a fairly open plan flow past large windows into a landscape, blurring the boundary between inside and outside in approaches I have seldom attempted since. Episodic in its organization, the plan unravels to reveal a sequence of spaces, some daringly configured. Skylights and clerestories create screenlike walls, slicing the house so that even rooms intended as static transform into visually kinetic places of passage.

With its Modernist space continuum, this is the house for which my Yale training had prepared me. But once the house was built, I saw problems with that approach that profoundly affected virtually all of my future residential work. Though I faced and conquered spatial as well as technical complexities galore in this house—such as the glazed conservatory with its flat skylight and the large exterior windows that slide into wall pockets to create a remarkably open feel—I learned things about what makes a house different from other building types, lessons for which the Yale approach had not prepared me.

For one thing, the spatial variety of the plan—with its surprising light sources, contrasting scales, and intricately framed views—is better suited to the wandering architectural tourist than to the owner and her guests sharing a quiet evening at home. Defined rooms and places of repose are in somewhat short supply in this design, as is the intimacy-yielding variety of scale that comes with more traditional vocabularies. I made some efforts in this direction—in consideration of the idea that the living room should be both "a goldfish bowl and a cave," a phrase that Paul Rudolph, another of my teachers at Yale whose influence on my work has been profound, would repeat to emphasize the need to provide for different moods and scales, I borrowed the inglenook of the nineteenth-century house. But without sufficient enclosure, the rooms could not achieve the intimacy the house so dearly craved.

Though the Westchester County Residence and its companion, the Lang House, did not represent a direction I would follow in residential architecture, it was an important first step in our nonresidential work that would lead to the Disney Casting Center at Walt Disney World (1987–1989) and the Feature Animation Building at Disney's Burbank studios (1991–1994). What the Westchester County Residence lacks in domesticity it makes up in spatial surprises, and it sits very well on its site. In fact, as I look back on it more than twenty years later, it is better than I remembered it—and, for all its uncharacteristic aspects, I list it among my best.

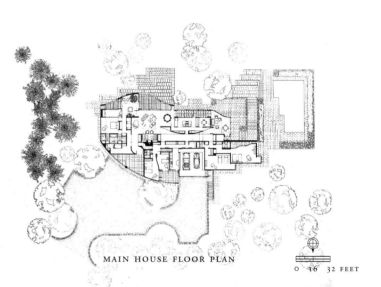

MAIN HOUSE FLOOR PLAN

0   16   32 FEET

GARDENER'S COTTAGE FLOOR PLAN

0   4   8   16 FEET

LEFT

FIRST ROW

Approach to house.

View of gardener's cottage from the west.

LEFT

SECOND ROW

View from the northwest.

View of gardener's cottage from the northeast.

BELOW

North facade detail.

ROBERT A. M. STERN: HOUSES

LEFT
*View from changing room
entrance to the west.*

BELOW
*Hallway looking
toward living room.*

LEFT
Living room.

BELOW
Master bedroom.

FIRST OVERLEAF
*View looking up from
changing-room entrance.*

SECOND OVERLEAF
Twilight view of south facade.

GREENWICH POOLHOUSE

GREENWICH, CONNECTICUT 1973–1974 After the tight-budget intensity of the Lang House, the liberating opportunity presented by this poolhouse was welcoming. Maybe the generosity of my clients and their request for something boldly different led me to go a bit far, but I remain proud of this early work that combines exuberance and vigorous geometry with cultural rootedness. In its formal freedom the Greenwich Poolhouse is very much a work of its time, very much in the tradition of spatial gymnastics that was important in my early training. The liberated shingled surfaces virtually explode apart to create an airy, tentlike pavilion, bathed in light from above.

My ambitions for this poolhouse were the highest, as recorded in an essay I wrote to accompany its July 1975 publication in *Architectural Record,* an essay that I now regard as pretentious—but what young architect's early writings aren't pretentious? Rereading that piece, I find that I managed to invoke the work of virtually every architect I admired, living or dead. Of course my wordy show of historical erudition was intended to rebuke the establishment, which still clung to the false ideal of heroic originality. Showing that buildings from the past could release the imagination in the present now seems pretty commonplace, but in the early 1970s it was a provocation. All things considered, however, perhaps the combination of the history lesson and the spatial and formal release of this design was just a bit too much.

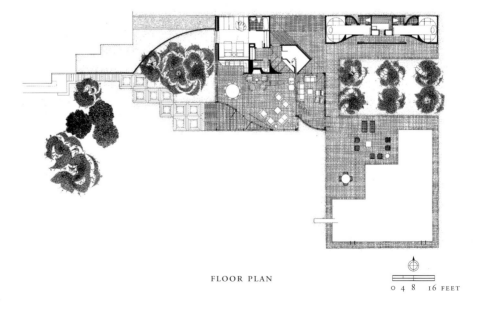

FLOOR PLAN

0 4 8   16 FEET

BELOW LEFT
View from the west.

BELOW RIGHT
View from the southwest.

RIGHT
FIRST ROW
Kitchen.
Living room.
Living room.

SECOND ROW
Living room.
Living room.
Bedroom.

THIRD ROW
Changing room.
Bedroom.
Changing room.

NEW YORK CITY TOWNHOUSE

NEW YORK, NEW YORK 1974–1975 To be able to design one of the very few new townhouses built in New York since the early 1930s was a great opportunity. Though the site was nothing if not prominent, it had the disadvantage of being awkwardly squeezed between large apartment blocks. In keeping with the compositional order of the surroundings, the facade was treated in the Classical manner—sort of. That is to say, this was one of my earliest attempts to come to terms with Classicism, or at least the grammar of Classicism, but with the exception of the imitations of pilasters framing the big windows and a few details, I shied away from all but the most primitive components of that tradition. I was timid, using an abstract gridding to suggest the time-honored schema of base, shaft, and capital. A recessed horizontal band of windows suggests a frieze that lines up with key band courses on the adjoining facades. Modernist abstraction injects irony into the gradual progression from solid to void in the vertical plane, capped by a cornice that appears to be suspended from above. Formally self-denying, the facade nonetheless engages its neighbors in some sort of dialogue, however inarticulate our contribution to the conversation might be, and evokes images of the grand townhouse tradition of which I so much wanted this house to be a part.

Under the influence of the 1920s Cubist work of Le Corbusier, which informed many of the apartment renovations that were the principal part of my practice at the time, any hint of Classical order that might have been found on the exterior was banished inside in favor of a Modernist *promenade architecturale* that leads from the entrance hall up to the master bedroom suite. Instead of rooms, a series of open platforms wraps a central atrium. A sinuous, cabinetlike wall of varying thickness directs the path of movement and defines places of repose in an interior landscape that is probably too full of spatial variety, not to mention razzle-dazzle.

RIGHT
View of living room with seating area below.

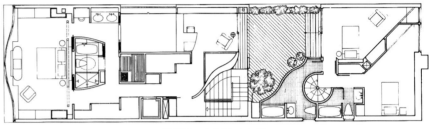

THIRD FLOOR PLAN

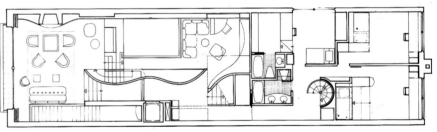

SECOND FLOOR PLAN

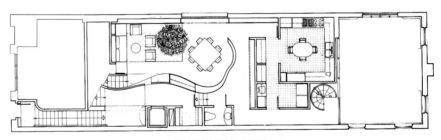

FIRST FLOOR PLAN

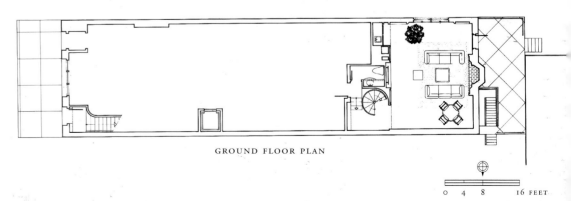

GROUND FLOOR PLAN

0   4   8   16 FEET

LEFT
Second-floor hallway.

BELOW
Second-floor hallway.

BELOW
First-floor hallway.

RIGHT
FIRST ROW
Study.
View of dining room from seating area.
View of seating area from dining room.
Second-floor hallway.

SECOND ROW
View of living room with entrance stairway on the right.
View of study from living room with dining room below.
View of living room from study.
View from living room with dining room below.

THIRD ROW
Stairway to master bedroom.
Master bedroom.
Living room detail.
Atrium.

FOURTH ROW
Atrium.
Powder room.
Powder room.
Basement play room.

LLEWELLYN PARK RESIDENCE

LLEWELLYN PARK, NEW JERSEY 1979–1981 This project called for the addition of an indoor swimming pool as well as the renovation of a fifty-year-old Georgian house designed by Edgar Williams. Normally I would not choose to bulldoze my way through such a substantial house as this. But Williams's design, a version of the so-called Wrenaissance style of Sir Edwin Lutyens, had a plan so conventional that it seemed to cry out for reconfiguration. We replaced the boxy, underlit rooms of the interior with space-defining screen walls threaded within a grid of structural columns. As a result of our work, a traditional house of 1929 was "modernized" using compositional strategies that were already fifty years old, leading me to conclude that "modern" wasn't modern anymore.

In contrast to the freedom of the renovated plan, the stone-and-glass poolhouse, designed as a basement-level extension, was very modern—that is to say "post-modern." In a direct response to the character of the original house, albeit in an exaggerated way, the pool was treated as a grotto or *nymphaeum;* mediating between nature and artifice, it marks a transition between the house, its terraces, and the garden. By virtue of its massive columns and thick masonry walls as well as the proto-Classical inspiration of its highly theatrical forms, the poolhouse provides a setting that is both primordial and entertaining.

The design is full of jokes, which is, after all, appropriate for a good-time space. The palm-tree columns supporting the terrace suggest a desert oasis. John Nash created such columns at the Royal Pavilion in Brighton (1822), as did Hans Hollein in a travel office in Vienna (1978) in order to trigger pleasant thoughts of exotic, sun-filled landscapes. The tile walls lend the room a subaqueous character. Faux-marble pilasters of almost archaic character complement various high-tech strategies employed to capture solar heat and natural light, making it possible to enjoy the pleasures of an earthly paradise while the garden outside is buried in snow. The intention everywhere is to deceive in a knowing way: the architects make the jokes, but the swimmers get to laugh.

RIGHT
Side pavilion.

OVERLEAF
South facade.

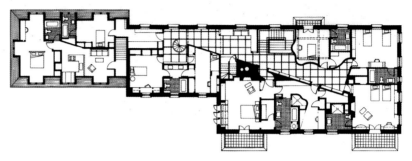

SECOND FLOOR PLAN

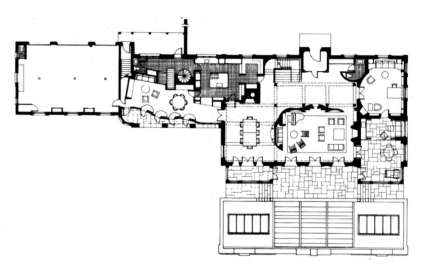

FIRST FLOOR PLAN

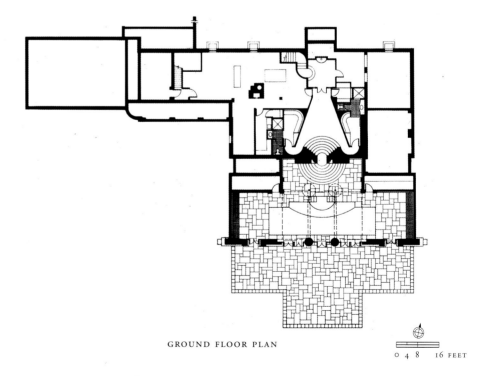

GROUND FLOOR PLAN

0 4 8 16 FEET

LEFT
*View of dining room
from entrance hall.*

BELOW
Entrance hall.

BELOW
*Poolhouse corridor and
vestibule.*

RIGHT
Poolhouse vestibule.

FIRST OVERLEAF
View of pool from vestibule.

SECOND OVERLEAF
Pool.

THIRD OVERLEAF
Pool.

FOURTH OVERLEAF
Night view of pool.

POINTS OF VIEW

MOUNT DESERT ISLAND, MAINE 1975–1976;
1992–1993 The prospect of designing this house on Mount Desert Island, Maine, was first broached to me when I was working on the Greenwich Poolhouse for the same clients. I very much hoped the job would come my way, not only because I liked my clients but also because of my admiration of the island's rich tradition of Shingle Style houses. To my disappointment, my clients bought a spectacular point of waterfront land that included a recently completed, teepee-like Modernist house. But Maine being Maine, nature had its way, and on a very cold, windy March night, before they could move in, the house was consumed by fire. When I was told about the disaster, I fell impelled to vouchsafe that I had not been skulking around the island wreaking havoc. In any case, as the debris was being cleared away from the site, in my head I was formulating plans for what the new house might be.

The result, Points of View, completed in 1976, was my first fully formed Shingle Style house, and therefore very important for me. Looking back, however, I can see just how tentative was my grasp on the design issues involved. Efforts to evoke the traditional Shingle Style can be seen in the covered entry porch that suggests a porte cochere; in the stair to the second floor that plots its own landscape for sitting as well as for walking; and in the schedule of interior finishes and details that follow time-honored construction techniques.

The living room, which also served for dining, was envisioned as a living hall, a broad, multifunction space lying between the stairs and the view. A local craftsman created a beautiful granite fireplace. But in a lingering Modernist gesture, four round metal columns were left in all their naked glory to denote the principal sitting area. (These have since been incorporated into paneled walls that have helped to stabilize the perhaps too "movemented" and certainly pointlessly severe space. The open porch has been closed in to create a separate dining room.)

Sixteen years after completing Points of View, I welcomed the opportunity to make some significant changes, correcting a technical problem at the entrance by creating a new entrance hall at a half level that leads to a new study on one side; and adding a large screened porch that extends the house into the landscape, its gently curving plan grabbing a long view of the water. With its asymmetrical and picturesque forms—the prominent stone chimney at the screened porch, the large central gable and oriel window of the new entry hall, and the layered gable of the new entrance porch—the reconfigured house seems to overcome the stiff regularity and symmetry of the original.

While renovating Points of View, I was asked to add on to a playhouse on the property that had been designed by another architect. This addition principally housed an International squash court, as well as a bowling alley with one standard and one candlepin lane. The addition matches the roofline of the original building to create a paired-gable entrance facade, but the bowling alley is handled as a distinctive wing, inspired by stable buildings of the 1880s.

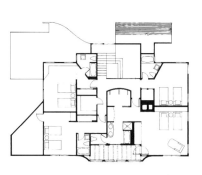

PHASE I SECOND FLOOR PLAN

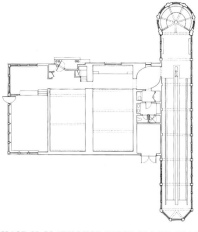

PHASE II PLAYHOUSE FIRST FLOOR PLAN

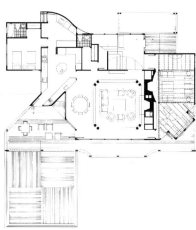

PHASE I FIRST FLOOR PLAN

0 4 8   16 FEET

PHASE II FIRST FLOOR PLAN

0 8 16 FEET

ROBERT A. M. STERN: HOUSES

LEFT TOP
*Principal facade of
original house.*

LEFT BOTTOM
*View of the original house
from the northeast.*

BELOW TOP
View from the southeast.

BELOW BOTTOM
Entrance (north) facade.

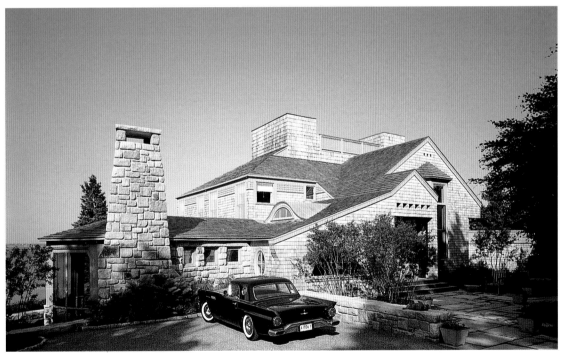

ROBERT A. M. STERN: HOUSES

BELOW TOP
*View of playhouse
from the northwest.*

BELOW BOTTOM
*View of playhouse
entrance from the southwest.*

RIGHT
*North facade of bowling
alley wing.*

LEFT
International squash court.

BELOW
Viewing gallery of
International squash court.

BELOW TOP
Bowling alley detail.

BELOW BOTTOM
Bowling alley.

RIGHT
Bowling alley seating area.

OVERLEAF
Twilight view of bowling alley wing from the north.

RESIDENCE AT CHIL-MARK

MARTHA'S VINEYARD, MASSACHUSETTS 1979–1983

The Residence at Chilmark marked a return to the themes—but not the crudities—of the Wiseman House (1965–1967; see page 12). One of our key houses in the Shingle Style, the Residence at Chilmark is marked by strongly contrasted archetypal and vernacular forms.

The house faces the sea at Menemsha, the only public place from which the house can be glimpsed, and that at a considerable distance. The visitor approaches the house from the landward side across a crest, and beyond the crest, on axis, is presented with a boldly proclaimed pediment suggesting the front facade of a temple. Punctured by an oversized oculus

window, the temple allusion is under-
cut by an asymmetrically placed,
recessed entrance. In addition to the
house-as-temple design story, we also
set out—and I think succeeded—to
create a modern house reflecting the
unconscious vernacular of a simple,
timeless way of building. (This knowledge and ability have largely disap-
peared from the building trades and,
irony of ironies, have been relearned
by university-trained architects.)
Notable manifestations of this vernacular include the flaring shingle-
skirting as well as the square posts
that carry the low-pitched, multi-
dormered hipped roof, which seems
to float above the porches.

As with many of our residences that
enjoy panoramic views, the Residence
at Chilmark is treated as a long wall, a
metaphor for the transition from the
everyday world of work and travel to
the arcadia of private garden and
views. Upon entering the house, the
view is held back by a solid wall that
angles to the living room, an expansive low-ceilinged space that focuses
the eye both inward to the inglenook
and outward to the sea.

RIGHT TOP
View from the southeast.

RIGHT BOTTOM
*Deck at northwest
corner of house.*

FIRST OVERLEAF
Entrance (east) facade.

SECOND OVERLEAF
West facade.

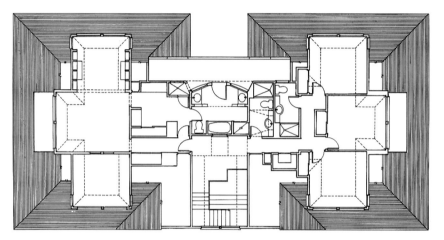

SECOND FLOOR PLAN

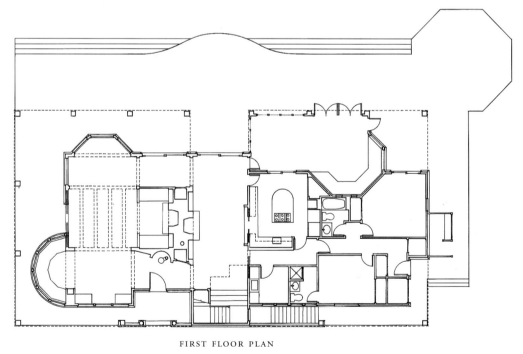

FIRST FLOOR PLAN

0   4   8   16 FEET

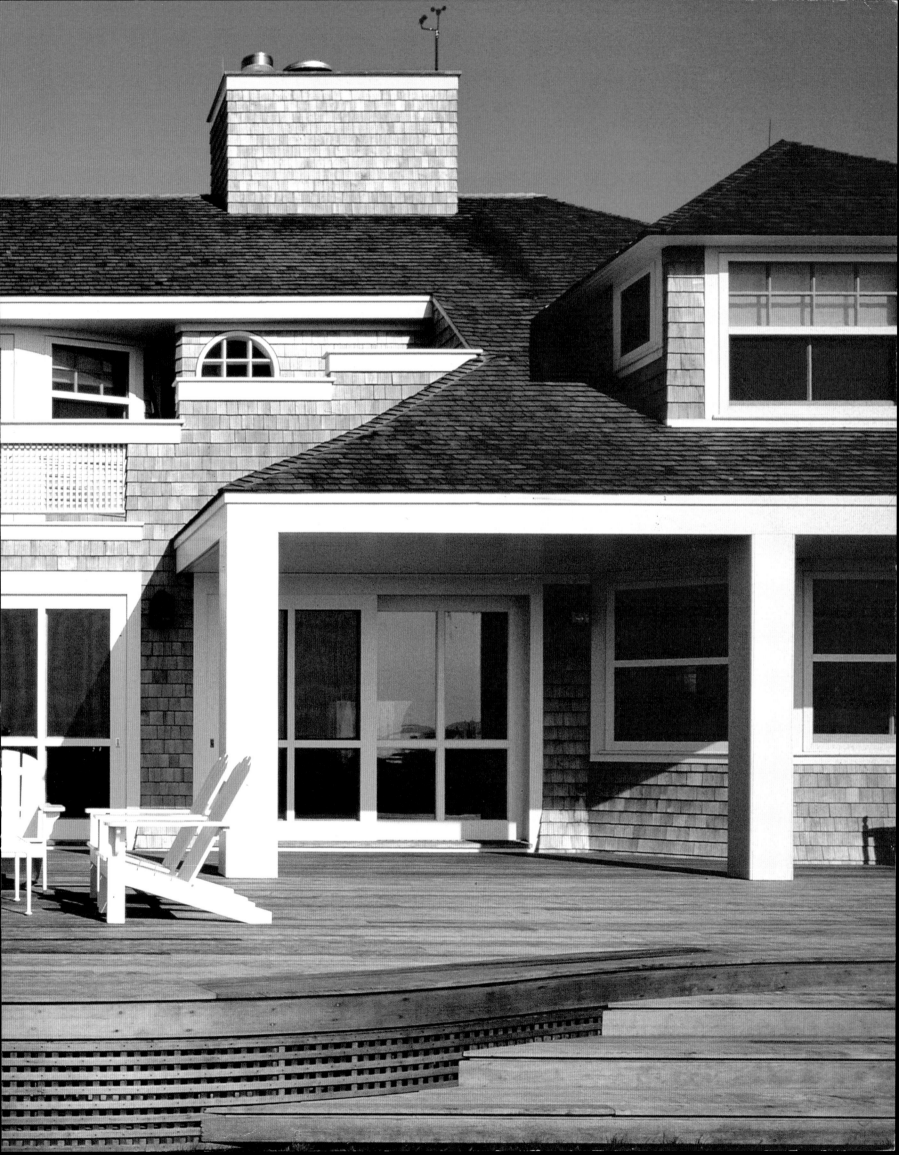

LEFT TOP
View from the northwest.

LEFT BOTTOM
*View from master
bedroom to the north.*

BELOW TOP
View to the north.

BELOW BOTTOM
*View from porch
to the northwest.*

LEFT
Stairway.

BELOW TOP
Living room.

BELOW BOTTOM
Master bedroom.

BELOW
Living room.

RIGHT
Dining room and stairway.

OVERLEAF
*Twilight view from
the southwest.*

RESIDENCE AT FARM NECK

MARTHA'S VINEYARD, MASSACHUSETTS 1980–1983

Located on a virtually flat site bordered at one edge by high trees and open on the other three sides to neighboring house lots, a golf course, and a distant water view, this house follows on the heels of the Residence at Chilmark in adapting the temple facade to a more complex program. Jointly commissioned by two families, sometimes the house would be home to one family or the other, and other times both families would be in residence and would require privacy from one another. This complicated program led to a puzzlelike layout with spaces wrapping around each other in both plan and cross section, but in the end I think we succeeded in creating a cohesive whole.

The dominating superimposed gables at first glance appear to have been inspired by McKim, Mead and White's Low House in Bristol, Rhode Island (1887); in fact, the superimposition of a small and large gable was derived from Grosvenor Atterbury's less archetypal Swayne House in Shinnecock Hills, New York (circa 1898). The clarity of the gable form lends the house an imposing scale, which is enhanced by the near symmetry of the principal facade and the pronounced silhouette of the chimneys and dormers. On the entrance side, the projection of a smaller gabled wing implies an entrance court and provides intimacy of scale. The projecting bay windows open the interior to the view, while the extensive use of mullioned windows helps to enrich the impact of the vast site by framing it.

RIGHT TOP
View from the southwest.

RIGHT BOTTOM
View from the southeast.

OVERLEAF
Entrance (north) facade.

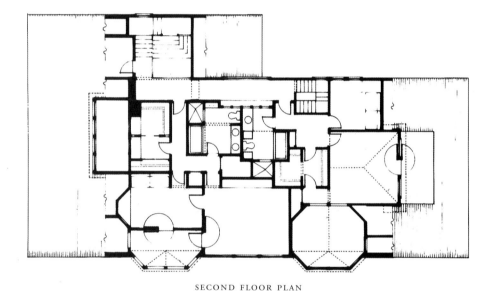

SECOND FLOOR PLAN

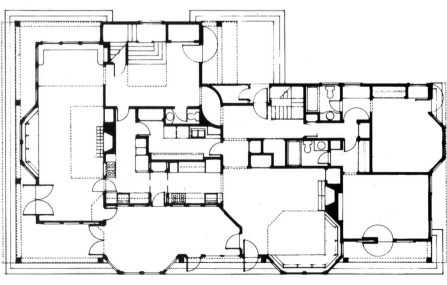

FIRST FLOOR PLAN

0   4   8   16 FEET

LEFT
Staircase.

BELOW
Living room.

OVERLEAF
Family room.

BELOW
*View from bedroom
over family room.*

RIGHT
Second-floor hallway.

ROBERT A. M. STERN: HOUSES

LEFT
*View from porch
to the southeast.*

BELOW
Master bedroom porch.

OVERLEAF
Twilight view of south facade.

BELOW
*Twilight view of
approach to house.*

RIGHT
Night view of entrance.

TREADWAY HOUSE

SOUTHAMPTON, NEW YORK 1983–1985 The Treadway House is another in our series of temple-fronted shingled houses, but is less complex and distinguished by a gently raked roof to help tie it to the relentlessly flat landscape, formerly fallow farmland. Only the large gable breaks through the roofline on the north elevation, providing a large-scale element to announce the entrance. On the south side, the roof is interrupted by the bedroom dormers and by the two-story bay of the living room, whose elliptical window looks toward the sea like a giant eye.

The first-floor plan provides an informal connection between the primary rooms; like a traditional Shingle Style hall, the living room connects the study, dining room, and second floor. The covered porch that surrounds these spaces becomes a screened room at the southwest corner. The stepped arrangement of the entry gable's windows follows the path of the staircase inside, and upstairs a generous landing connects the master bedroom suite and the children's rooms. From the landing, a second staircase leads to the third-floor studio, which offers panoramic views of the distant fields and ocean.

RIGHT
View from porch to the south.

OVERLEAF
Entrance (northwest) facade.

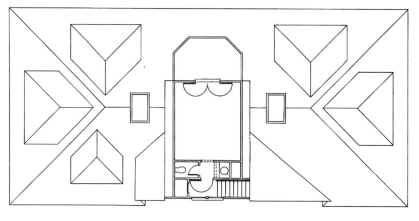

THIRD FLOOR PLAN

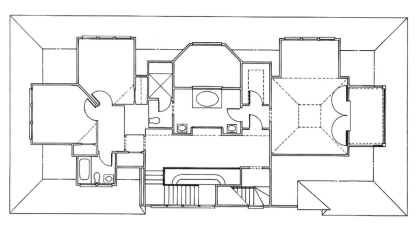

SECOND FLOOR PLAN

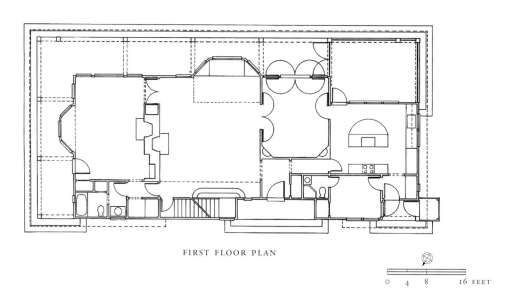

FIRST FLOOR PLAN

0   4   8   16 FEET

LEFT
Stairway.

BELOW
Living room detail.

FIRST OVERLEAF
Southeast facade.

SECOND OVERLEAF
View from porch to the north.

RESIDENCE AT HARD- SCRABBLE

EAST HAMPTON, NEW YORK 1983–1985 Approached along a winding drive that terminates in a clearly defined forecourt carved out of the woods, the Residence at Hardscrabble confronts the arriving visitor with a pedimentlike gable that gives no hint of the intimate spaces and sweeping views that lie beyond, where broad porches open up to spectacular views of farmland and ocean seen from just below the crest of eastern Long Island's highest ridge.

The Residence at Hardscrabble is, in some ways, the most mature version to date of the Wiseman House, my first house in Montauk, coming as close to vernacular naturalness as any we have yet achieved.

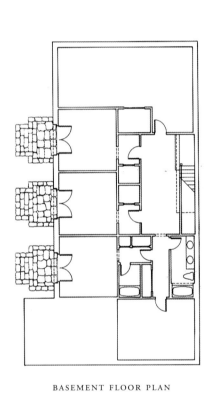

BASEMENT FLOOR PLAN

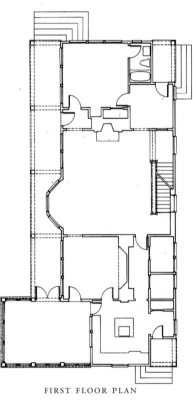

FIRST FLOOR PLAN

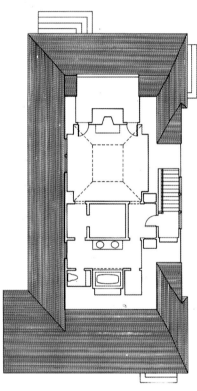

SECOND FLOOR PLAN

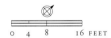

0   4   8   16 FEET

LEFT
*View of stairway
from entrance hall.*

BELOW
Stairway.

FIRST OVERLEAF
Master bedroom detail.

SECOND OVERLEAF
View from porch to the south.

LAWSON HOUSE

EAST QUOGUE, NEW YORK 1979–1981 Nothing pleases me more than the knowledge that the Lawson House has become an icon of contemporary seaside architecture. Set along the ocean on a narrow lot, the house marks a milestone in our ongoing effort to connect the present to the past. On the one hand, the Lawson House belongs to the long tradition of almost shacklike beach cottages, vacation residences that proliferated along the East Coast from the 1880s through the 1920s. With their stylistic simplicity and direct use of appropriate materials, these cottages have successfully and indelibly defined seaside summers for so many people. On the other hand, it is a monumentally scaled—if not monumentally sized—villa with distinct Palladian pretensions.

The position of the Lawson House at
the edge of a dune made it possible to
tuck three small guest bedrooms at
grade in the rear. The overscaled
stoop leading up to the main floor
provides an inviting porch from
which to observe the sunset across the
bay, while the primary living rooms,
located just below the crest of the
dune, face the broad expanse of sea
and sand to the south. The master
bedroom, which fills the cavity of the
generously pitched roof, looks to the
sea through a large, Roman-inspired
thermal window. Though the eroded
configuration of the principal floor
responds to the particular considera-
tions of site, view, and solar orientation, the fundamentally symmetrical
organization of the mass is intended
to give the house a dignity and iconic
clarity of its own—an object of calm
amid helter-skelter.

I was very pleased with the results,
especially with the marriage of high
Classicism and grandma's house. But
when I overheard two women walking on the beach engaging in a debate
over whether the house's flaring roofs
were Japanese or Chinese in origin,
I learned one important lesson:
meaning is as much in the eye of the
beholder as in the mind of the
architect. Still, for those women the
house worked as I had hoped—it
made connections.

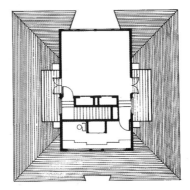

MEZZANINE LEVEL FLOOR PLAN

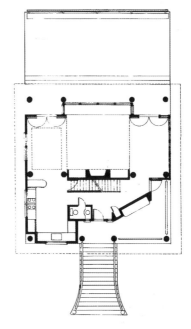

FIRST FLOOR PLAN

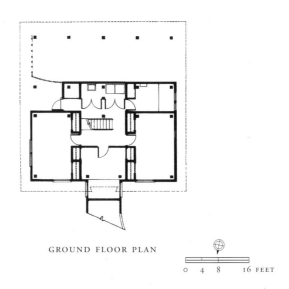

GROUND FLOOR PLAN

0   4   8   16 FEET

LEFT

View from the southwest.

BELOW

South facade.

OVERLEAF

Dining area.

LEFT TOP
Living room.

LEFT BOTTOM
*View from stair
hall to the west.*

BELOW
Kitchen.

FIRST OVERLEAF
Master bedroom.

SECOND OVERLEAF
*Twilight view from
the southwest.*

LEFT
*View from the southeast
(house at top right).*

RESIDENCE ON RUSSIAN HILL

SAN FRANCISCO, CALIFORNIA 1985–1989 There is much to be learned from rebuilding old houses. In our early renovations, the existing houses prepared us for new work. More recently, the new work has sometimes helped us to grapple with problems posed by the old. Reconstruction need not confine the architect to a literal recapitulation of the past, and I have learned that neither must the new work be in obvious contrast with the old. The freedom to interpret does not necessarily mean that a "modern" style overlay is appropriate. Rather, as in this case, reconstruction can create spaces and put in place details that were not original to the house but could have—and perhaps should have—been. The past *can* be improved upon.

The history of this house is worth retelling. Built as an unpretentious two-story farmhouse set atop Russian Hill, it began life in 1865 when San Francisco was barely more than a village. Most of the hill, including the house, was later acquired by Horace Livermore. In the late 1880s, Livermore rented the house to two young architects, Willis Polk and Addison Mizner, who renovated the ground floor. When the Livermore family chose to occupy the house around 1890, they evicted their tenants and added a third floor, calling upon Polk to spruce up the interiors of the boxlike mass of the expanded house. Polk obliged by adding Classical details, some of which are still in place on the ground floor. The house, like most of its neighbors on the hill, escaped the ravages of the earthquake and fire that devastated San Francisco in 1906. In the 1930s, William Wilson Wurster, another of San Francisco's famous architects specializing in houses, stripped most of the design bare in keeping with his International Style Modernism aesthetic. When our clients bought the house in 1985, however, it had been converted into two apartments, and any signs of stylish modernity had long since given way to shabbiness.

This extensive reconstruction and expansion consisted of two significant compositional strategies: the addition of a picturesque tower, placed asymmetrically at the northwest corner, creating a dramatic entry and providing critically needed space on the top floor; and the insertion of a *promenade architecturale* that leads guests from the street past the "invisible" intermediate bedroom level to the top floor, where the rooms for entertaining are located to take advantage of uncommonly beautiful views. Although the austere shingled idiom of the original house is retained in this reconstruction, the new tower and the detailing of the entrance porch enhance the silhouette and add vitality.

The new outside staircase combines with new interior arrangements—most notably the stair hall and the twenty-by-thirty-four-foot-long vaulted living room that rises fourteen feet between relocated roof trusses—to constitute one of our most satisfying spatial sequences (of course, the climax of a drop-dead view of San Francisco doesn't hurt).

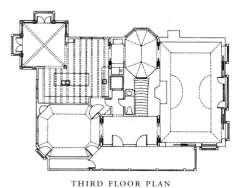

THIRD FLOOR PLAN

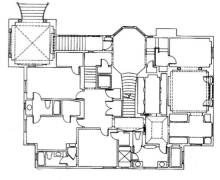

SECOND FLOOR PLAN

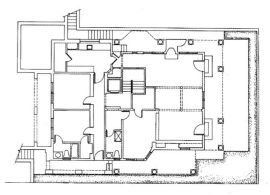

FIRST FLOOR PLAN

0   4   8   16 FEET

LEFT

East facade detail.

BELOW

View from the northwest.

OVERLEAF

View from the west.

LEFT
Principal stairway.

BELOW
Entrance hall.

OVERLEAF
Living room.

LEFT

Master bathroom.

BELOW

*View from roof garden
to the southeast, toward
downtown San Francisco.*

EAST HAMPTON RESIDENCE

EAST HAMPTON, NEW YORK 1980–1983 In undertaking this house, my growing commitment to modern traditionalism faced a key test. Located in the heart of East Hampton, a traditional "summer colony," this residence was the first of our Shingle Style houses to be built in a neighborhood dominated by classic Shingle Style works of the nineteenth century. The site, a former side garden for another house, contained established planting as well as a guest house and swimming pool, so our house was forced close to the street to preserve the landscape. There was literally no place to hide and our new house had to work with an existing context in which it would be a quite visible component.

Despite a high hedge that created some privacy, the house had to function as a wall to the street, though we would punctuate the barrier with a pedimented porch ornamented with abstract openwork. We could be freer on the garden side, where we elevated the boxlike mass of the house onto a brick base to form the floor of the screened porches as well as of the covered terrace outside the living room. We counterpointed the cubic structure with the familiar Shingle Style feature of a conical tower, but handled this element in an unorthodox way, pulling it away from the mass to admit light and air at the top.

Applied to the relatively straightforward mass, the ironic handling of key elements and details—the entrance porch, the eyebrow dormers, the latticed garden-facing loggia, and the detached conical turret—accentuates the dialogue between past and present. This mode of interpreting and reshaping traditional elements also demonstrates our ability to create a new building that reflects both specific memories as well as the desire to make something of our own.

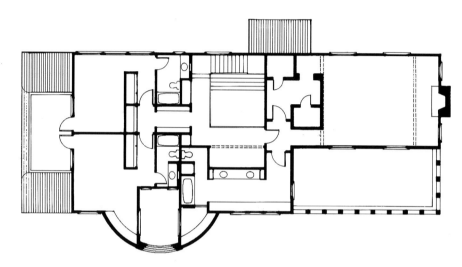

SECOND FLOOR PLAN

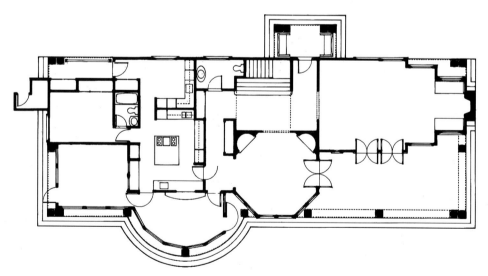

FIRST FLOOR PLAN

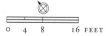

0   4   8   16 FEET

LEFT
Tower.

BELOW TOP
View from the southeast.

BELOW BOTTOM
View from the southwest.

BELOW
Stairway.

RIGHT
*Stair hall looking
toward living room.*

OVERLEAF
Stairway.

LEFT
View of porch from second floor.

BELOW TOP
Living room.

BELOW BOTTOM
Dining room looking toward porch.

MARBLEHEAD RESIDENCE

MARBLEHEAD, MASSACHUSETTS 1984–1987 Like the East Hampton Residence, the Marblehead Residence does not in any way represent the ideal of the house as temple. Its boxlike mass was instead shaped in response to program and landscape so that the final result seems the natural outgrowth of its oddly shaped lot. Though the site slopes down to a spectacular water view, its northward orientation challenged us in pulling as much southern light into the year-round house as possible. The difficulty of this goal was compounded by deed requirements guaranteeing sight lines for neighboring houses. The resultant L-shaped plan literally grabs for the sun. The cruciform living room, centered around interwoven planes and volumes, combines with the double-height entry hall and turreted stair to foster a relaxed interior architecture consonant with the exterior's relative informality.

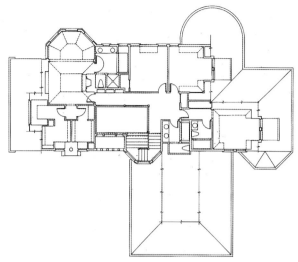

SECOND FLOOR PLAN

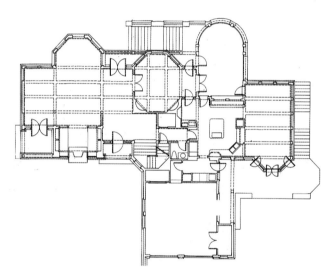

FIRST FLOOR PLAN

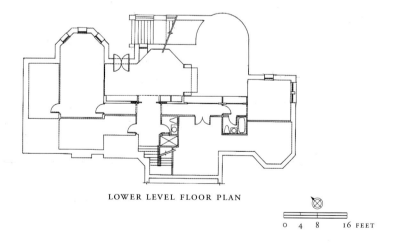

LOWER LEVEL FLOOR PLAN

0   4   8   16 FEET

SUN-STONE

QUOGUE, NEW YORK 1984–1987 Despite its strictly rural character, the Sunstone site can be described in almost urban terms: it is located at the nearly right-angled intersection where Stone Creek empties out into Shinnecock Bay. Though the site was large, the usual pressures of solar orientation and view were further complicated by a deed restriction protecting the views of another house behind it. Entered along a drive that winds through the woods, the house marks a point of landscape transition; behind, broad lawns and formal gardens spread down to the water. The boxlike main mass of the house is counterpointed by strong diagonal wings, with a two-story lighthouselike tower at the southwest corner. The diagonal extension frames the entry facade and makes the

house appear smaller than it really is. A
vernacular gambreled roof sweeps down
over encircling verandas, while a
Classical entry portico and Palladian
window announce the entry hall, a generous room leading from front to back
in the manner of Georgian houses.

RIGHT
Entrance.

OVERLEAF
Southeast facade.

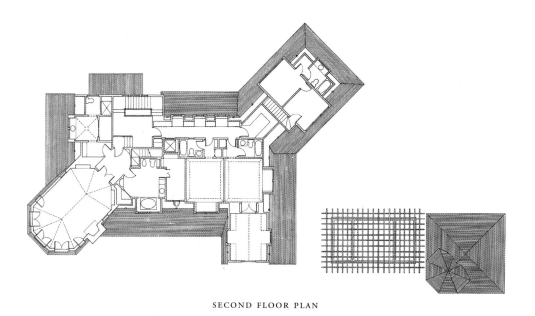

SECOND FLOOR PLAN

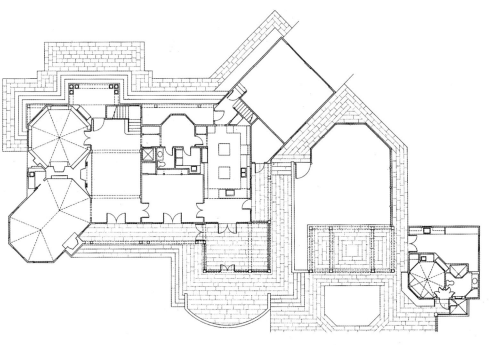

FIRST FLOOR PLAN

0   4 8   16 FEET

ROBERT A. M. STERN: HOUSES

LEFT
View from the southeast.

BELOW LEFT
*View of pool area from
widow's walk.*

BELOW RIGHT
*View of pergola and
poolhouse from widow's walk.*

ROBERT A. M. STERN: HOUSES

LEFT

FIRST ROW

Poolhouse detail.

Entrance detail.

SECOND ROW

Entrance detail.

Entrance detail.

BELOW

View from the east.

LEFT
Library detail.

BELOW TOP
Kitchen.

BELOW BOTTOM
*View of entrance hall with
library on the right.*

LEFT
Master bedroom detail.

BELOW
Master bedroom.

OVERLEAF
View from the south.

RED OAKS

COHASSET, MASSACHUSETTS 1992–1995 Originally built as a summer residence in 1906 for a Boston family, Red Oaks changed hands only twice before being acquired by our clients. Photos provided by one of the previous owners reveal that the house had already taken on a ramshackle quality in the 1950s; by 1992 it was an absolute wreck. The placement of the house on a forty-foot-high granite outcropping that commands a view of Little Harbor, around which lies the town of Cohasset, however, was incomparable.

The house was too boxy to be classified as Shingle Style, and too irregular to be called Georgian; perhaps Colonial Revival would best characterize it stylistically. The main block was flanked by an angled service wing to the northeast and a ballroom to the west. The ballroom had probably been added on to the original house. The detailing both inside and out was rather spare. The only features that everyone agreed should be saved were the front door and the main staircase. The ballroom, in many ways the nicest room in the house, took up the best flat land on the site, and so was taken down, but with some regret.

Removal of the ballroom opened up a wonderful west-facing view for the new living room, and a formal garden and pool took its place. Bay windows and dormers were added. The service wing was extended with the addition of a porte cochere, which connects the house to a new garage and service courtyard. The plan was reconfigured so that the primary rooms are arranged around the entry hall, all opening one to the other.

Throughout the house we added details that might have been part of contemporaneously built houses. Inside, the entry hall was paneled and door surrounds adorned with carved dolphins and boats; the existing stairway, which is the hall's centerpiece, now looks more in keeping with its surroundings. To the visitor who doesn't know the now-renovated house's history, it looks as if a grand old house had merely been freshened up by new owners—in fact, that's exactly the effect we all had in mind.

RIGHT
Entrance.

OVERLEAF
North facade.

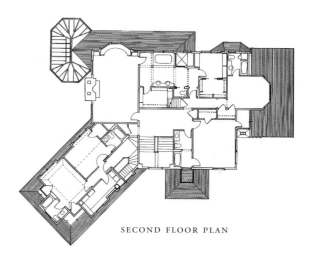

SECOND FLOOR PLAN

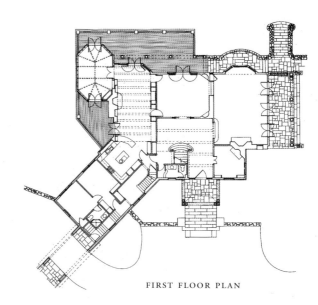

FIRST FLOOR PLAN

0 4 8   16 FEET

ROBERT A. M. STERN: HOUSES

ROBERT A. M. STERN: HOUSES

LEFT
*View from terrace
to the southwest.*

BELOW
*View from terrace
to the southeast.*

OVERLEAF
*Stair hall looking
toward living room.*

LEFT TOP
Kitchen.

LEFT BOTTOM
*Dining room looking
toward living room.*

BELOW TOP
Study.

BELOW BOTTOM
Master bedroom.

OVERLEAF
South facade.

LEFT
View of terrace from
library, with study above.

MILL NECK RESIDENCE

MILL NECK, NEW YORK 1981–1983 This important project offered new challenges and inaugurated a new set of investigations into the role of tradition in our architecture. Though on Long Island, the Mill Neck Residence is located away from the south-shore resorts and their Shingle Style context. It is instead set in a lushly landscaped north-shore neighborhood of big country houses, many designed between 1890 and 1940 by top architects. The commission came at a time when I was just beginning to be fascinated by the work of the English architect Sir Edwin Lutyens and his great American disciple, Harrie T. Lindeberg, who had, as it happened, designed many of the neighboring Mill Neck houses.

Lessons learned from Lutyens's Tigbourne Court in Witley, England (1899), as well as from Lindeberg's own house, built in 1927 on the grounds of the Piping Rock Club in Locust Valley, New York, helped to shape this house.

The Mill Neck Residence also reflects the interesting challenges posed by its beautiful site. There were some drawbacks—the flat, buildable area sat near a busy road, and the picturesquely framed view of Oyster Bay faces east rather than south or west, which I would have preferred. I had to find a way to incorporate the view while allowing the principal rooms to receive afternoon light. Although Lutyens's Tigbourne Court—with its remarkable entrance court close to the road, triple-gable facade, and surprising reorientation of the interior plan—was my guide, I moved away from the spatial contortions of Tigbourne's interior plan.

Our design strove for simplicity. A strong path of circulation along a broad, tall, light-filled hall acts as a spine off of which the major rooms open. To take advantage of the view, the living room faces east but is flooded with south light from a courtyard shared with the master bedroom and the stair hall. The stair hall, with deep niches over French doors on one side and a broad flight of stairs on the other, is in some ways the best room in the house. The hall leads past the vaulted living room, in its own pavilion, to a curving wall of glass that

allows the view to terminate in the garden while deflecting the path of circulation from the house's primary axis to a double-height, soot gray library that, like the dining room, enjoys west light.

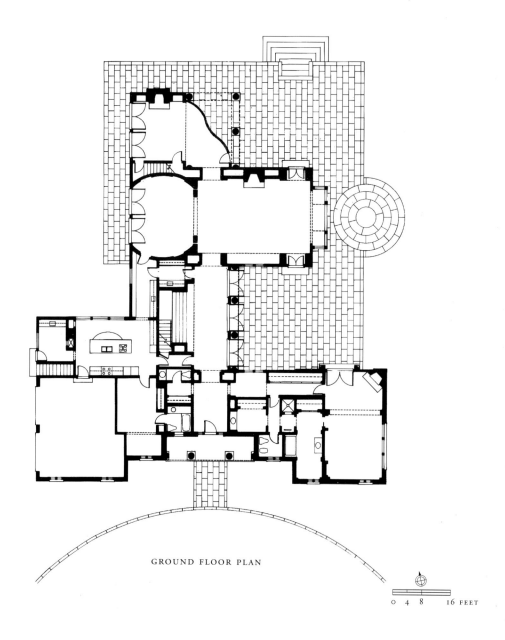

GROUND FLOOR PLAN

0 4 8   16 FEET

LEFT

*View of living room wing
from the southeast.*

BELOW

View from the northwest.

OVERLEAF

*Stair hall looking
toward library.*

HEWLETT HARBOR RESIDENCE

HEWLETT HARBOR, NEW YORK 1984–1988 Hewlett Harbor is a close suburb of New York, and its flat marshland encourages long, low houses that do not intrude on the larger landscape. Like the Mill Neck Residence, this Long Island house is not part of the south-shore resort scene. But unlike the lush Mill Neck setting, this site is flat and flanked by two very different contexts: in the front, a public street sits only thirty feet away; and in the back, a navigable channel opens through the tidal marshes to Hewlett Bay.

Drawing inspiration from Sir John
Soane's Pitzhanger Manor in Ealing,
England (1802), and C. R. Cockerell's
Ashmolean Museum in Oxford
(1845), as well as from the glamorous
Regency work of such 1930s stylists as
the English architect Oliver Hill, the
interior of the Hewlett Harbor
Residence continues the fully developed
Classical expression of the facade.
The distinct rooms do not sacrifice the
openness and spatial continuity that
many regard as a hallmark of contem-
porary interior design.

A sharp turn from the street leads to
the entry court, a precisely formed
exterior room defined by brick walls on
two sides and by the house facade on
the third. The west facade, which
overlooks the channel, is open to the
landscape with its long rows of French
doors. Though this perspective does
not have the columns and entablature
of the front, Classical order is nonetheless maintained; the terrace, bordered
by the house on three sides, acts as a
kind of double for the entrance court.

RIGHT
Approach to house.

OVERLEAF
View from the west.

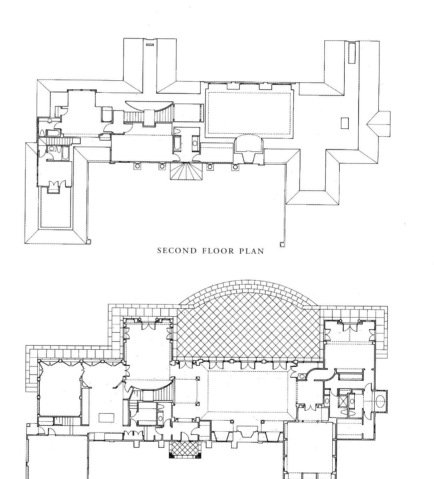

SECOND FLOOR PLAN

FIRST FLOOR PLAN

0   4   8   16 FEET

LEFT
View of dining room from living room.

BELOW
Living room and stairway.

ROBERT A. M. STERN: HOUSES

LEFT
View of living room
from entrance hall.
Living room.

BELOW
Living room.

RESIDENCE IN STAR- WOOD

ASPEN, COLORADO 1991–1996 In one of the most recent of our houses, we have returned to the source that inspired the Mill Neck Residence, Sir Edwin Lutyens's Tigbourne Court. Other aspects of Lutyens's work also guided us as we crafted a house that would seem at home in the mountain landscape while being more controlled in its geometry than is typical with Aspen houses, which tend to favor size over composition, resulting in massive roofs enveloping rambling, ill-defined interior spaces. Commanding sweeping views of the Roaring Fork Valley, our house is compact and geometrically resolved.

A curving drive negotiates the steep rise from the street and leads to a motor court, where the principal facade provides a decisive termination to the journey. The garages lie to one side behind a pergola screen, buried within the hill that rises steeply behind the site. Where Lutyens's triple-gable facade was sketchily interpreted at the Mill Neck Residence, here the investigation goes much deeper. The tawny granite exterior consists of carefully arranged pavilions and bays to help reduce the apparent mass of the house. A mottled purple-and-green slate roof and natural wood trim both serve to blend the house into its setting, as does the complex configuration of reflecting pool, retaining walls, wood pergolas, and terraces.

The interior of the house is organized on three floors, with the entrance and principal rooms on the middle level; the bedrooms above; and a spa suite on the bottom floor, including an indoor pool, billiards and weight rooms, and a racquetball court. Behind the north-facing, triple-gable entry, a two-story vaulted hall, paved and paneled in limestone, redirects the axis of movement to either side of the fireplace mass, around which the rooms are arranged. To the east the many stair landings trick the vertical scale. Three rooms—one a porch—are arranged enfilade across the front; the centerpiece living room frames the view to the west. The south-facing dining room enjoys a distant glimpse of Aspen Mountain across a precisely sculpted garden sheltered by the hill that rises past it.

RIGHT
View from the southwest.

FIRST OVERLEAF
View from the northwest.

SECOND OVERLEAF
View of south facade from garden overlook.

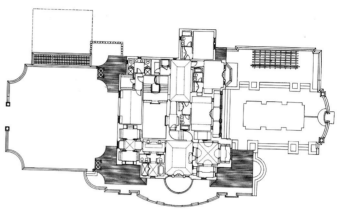

SECOND FLOOR PLAN

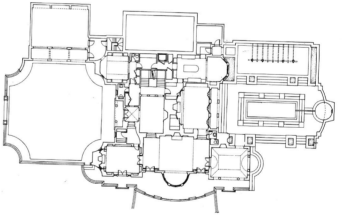

FIRST FLOOR PLAN

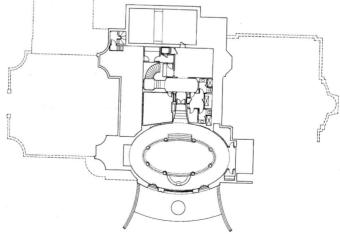

GROUND FLOOR PLAN

0   8   16 FEET

BELOW TOP
Terrace.

BELOW BOTTOM
Terrace.

RIGHT
View from porch toward garden overlook.

OVERLEAF
Porch.

LEFT
*Entrance hall looking
toward living room.*

BELOW LEFT
Entrance hall.

BELOW RIGHT
Upper stair hall.

FIRST OVERLEAF
Living room.

SECOND OVERLEAF
*Living room looking
toward library.*

THIRD OVERLEAF
*Library looking toward
living room.*

LEFT

Library.

BELOW LEFT

View of library from living room.

BELOW RIGHT

View from dining room toward garden overlook.

LEFT
Guest bedroom.

BELOW
Master bathroom.

ROBERT A. M. STERN: HOUSES

LEFT

Indoor pool.

BELOW

Indoor pool.

FIRST OVERLEAF

Twilight view of indoor pool.

SECOND OVERLEAF

Twilight view of west facade.

LEFT
*View of pool and ocean
from living room.*

DEAL
RESIDENCE

DEAL, NEW JERSEY 1982–1984 The architectural context of the site determined the decision to undertake an Italian-inspired villa. In the years between 1900 and 1930, in its guise as an American Riviera, this town became home to a rich array of Mediterranean work. Since the 1950s, many of these beautiful houses have been torn down and some "modernized," yet the Mediterranean presence is still strongly felt and a Shingle Style house would have been distinctly odd on the site.

Our small villa was directly inspired by Charles Platt's Italianate work, particularly High Court in Cornish, New Hampshire (1891), and by Frank Lloyd Wright's fully Classical design for the Winslow House in River Forest, Illinois (1893), though the earlier houses do not have the profusion of glass and the open, casually interrelated plan that seems to go hand in hand with beach-house design today. To work in a traditional style, however, does not mean to be strictly bound by it in its entirety. The new-old houses that I favor are not created in a spirit of archaeology. Instead, I attempt to forge a synthesis between traditional and modern ways of building so as to enrich the experience of architecture and enhance the sense of place.

RIGHT
Entrance hall.

FIRST OVERLEAF
Entrance.

SECOND OVERLEAF
East facade.

THIRD OVERLEAF
Living room.

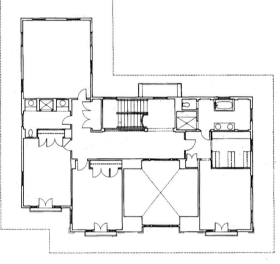

SECOND FLOOR PLAN

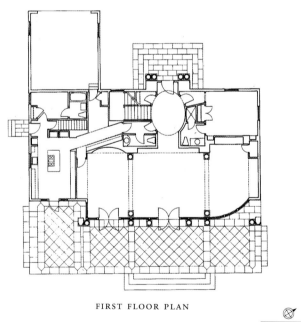

FIRST FLOOR PLAN

0   4   8   16 FEET

LEFT
Living room.

BELOW
Stair hall.

OVERLEAF
Twilight view of east facade.

VILLA IN NEW JERSEY

DEAL, NEW JERSEY 1983–1989 The Deal Residence led to a commission for a much larger house on a nearby site, offering an opportunity to realize what is perhaps the highest goal of Classical villa design: the complete integration of house and garden. The site, an oddly shaped two-and-a-half-acre parcel facing a busy shore road, is surrounded by much older houses, many of them early-twentieth-century Mediterranean-inspired villas.

The house and garden are gradually revealed; from the street, only a narrow facade can be glimpsed through the gate. The driveway circles beneath a porte cochere, where a garden wall conceals the service court beyond. A vestibule leads past a long cross-hall to an enfilade of the card, living, and dining rooms, each of which opens out to a pergola-shaded terrace overlooking a sunken court. Framed by telescoping walls and low trees at its outer side, the sunken court gives way to a view of sloping grass terraces. The terraces form a cross axis stretching from the house to a carved limestone fountain in the distance.

Beneath the pergola terrace, a grotto-like room housing the pool receives the axis of the sunken court and its forced perspective. The enclosed swimming pool is emblematic of the indoor-outdoor dialogue embodied within this house and its predecessors. The pool, for example, has its analogous double in the sunken court onto which it opens. Apsidal grottoes at both ends of the court offer a mannered commentary on the transitions between above- and belowground and between civilization and nature, a commentary that continues in the forced perspective of the court as it rises to the south.

In keeping with the Classical tradition, the gardens were subjected to the same geometrical discipline as the house. An orchestrated show of spring and summer flowers and evergreen planting in winter combine with the brick and bluestone paths to reveal the orderly organization of the site.

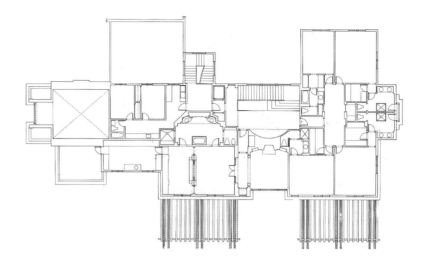

SECOND FLOOR PLAN

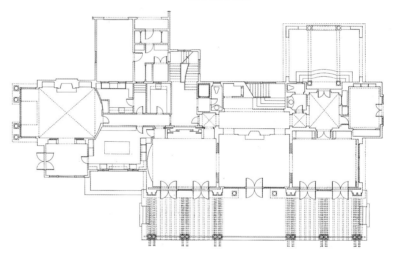

FIRST FLOOR PLAN

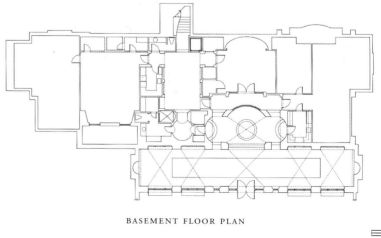

BASEMENT FLOOR PLAN

0 4 8   16 FEET

ROBERT A. M. STERN: HOUSES

LEFT TOP
Porte cochere.

LEFT BOTTOM
Approach to house.

BELOW TOP
Sunken garden.

BELOW BOTTOM
*View from terrace
toward stepped garden.*

BELOW
*View of south facade from
sunken garden.*

RIGHT
Pergola detail.

OVERLEAF
Stepped garden.

LEFT
View of flower garden from master bedroom terrace.

BELOW
View from master bedroom terrace.

OVERLEAF
View from flower garden toward pool pavilion.

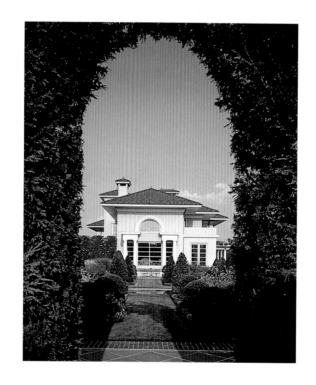

LEFT

Principal stairway.

BELOW

Entrance hall.

OVERLEAF

Living room.

BELOW
FIRST ROW
Dining room.
Sitting room in master
bedroom suite.

BELOW
SECOND ROW
Study.
Family room.

BELOW LEFT
Telephone room.

BELOW RIGHT
Master bedroom detail.

OVERLEAF
Rear stairway.

LEFT

FIRST ROW

Service console.

Dining room cabinet.

LEFT

SECOND ROW

*Side chair in master
bedroom suite.*

Breakfast room chair.

BELOW

Dresser.

OVERLEAF

Master bedroom suite.

LEFT TOP
Basement gallery.

LEFT BOTTOM
Entrance to indoor pool.

BELOW
Entrance to indoor pool.

FIRST OVERLEAF
Indoor pool.

SECOND OVERLEAF
Twilight view of indoor pool looking toward gardens.

THIRD OVERLEAF
Twilight view of pool pavilion.

RESIDENCE AT RIVER OAKS

HOUSTON, TEXAS 1988–1992 Houston is a comparatively new city, with no long-established architectural traditions. Though its leading suburban neighborhoods, such as River Oaks, abound in examples of virtually every style, the best houses are united by a respect for the city's difficult climate. No matter how different one house may look from another, the functional dispositions of the plans, with their porches, pergolas, and lush gardens, combine to create an overall coherence—a genuine sense of place.

Given the climate and the need to create green rather than flower-filled gardens, a house based on Italian themes seemed right. Creamy stuccoed walls and red-tile roofs work well during both times of intense sun and gray, rainy seasons in Houston. Pavilionated planning, local symmetries of massing, and a decorative vocabulary of Tuscan detail governed by Doric proportions help to lighten the effect and thereby reduce the apparent size of what is a large house.

Inside, fully expressed Classical detail is confined to principal interior rooms where a big scale seemed appropriate to a grand house. The two-story-high stair hall leads directly to a long hall opening to the garden. This axis joins the dining room, library, and family quarters on one end to the sumptuously ornamented and decorated living room on the other. The T-shaped living room permits light and air on three sides and allows for both large and small groups to gather comfortably.

The site features a northerly view of the Buffalo Bayou, but we nonetheless wanted to bring direct southern light into the principal rooms; courtyards were designed accordingly to buffer the south-facing rooms from the driveways. To the north, formal gardens extend the geometry of the house into the landscape. Even though the house is air-conditioned, the plan was conceived in an environmental spirit so that during the cooler months breezes can flow through it naturally. Enclosed by a screen tent to keep out the pine needles that continuously blow about, an outdoor swimming pool restates in a less jokey way themes first explored eleven years earlier at the Llewellyn Park Residence.

FIRST OVERLEAF
Entrance (south) facade.

SECOND OVERLEAF
View from garden to the south.

THIRD OVERLEAF
View to the northeast, with formal terrace in the foreground and tennis court in the distance.

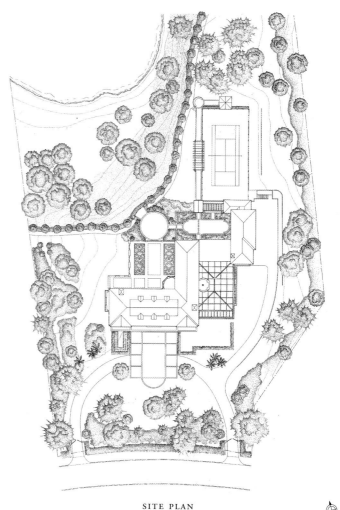

SITE PLAN

0 16 32 FEET

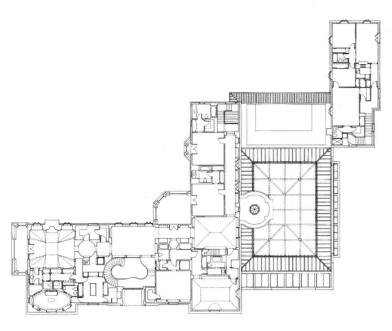

SECOND FLOOR PLAN

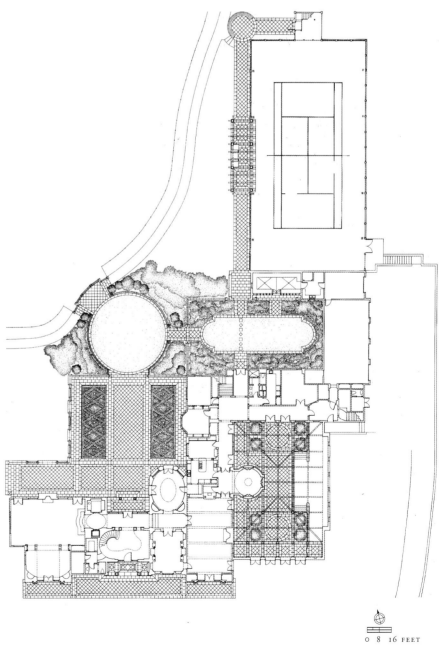

FIRST FLOOR PLAN

0 8 16 FEET

ROBERT A. M. STERN: HOUSES

LEFT TOP
Family room.

LEFT BOTTOM
Library.

BELOW
Master bathroom.

LEFT TOP
Screened-in pool.

LEFT BOTTOM
Twilight view of pool.

BELOW
*Twilight view of pool from
service hallway.*

OVERLEAF
Night view of entrance.

ELBERON RESIDENCE

ELBERON, NEW JERSEY 1985–1989 Located a mile or so away from the Villa in New Jersey, Elberon is also populated with Mediterranean villas, including the notable progenitor of the trend, Carrère & Hastings's villa for Murray Guggenheim (1903). The Elberon Residence looks not to Italy but to Spain for inspiration, in large part because the tradition of walled courtyards provided a way to shield outdoor space from a busy road. The simple stucco volumes, capped with red-tile roofs, suggest a Spanish farmhouse. The street-facing wall provides privacy while still admitting western light into a cloistered garden. Facing the ocean, the living and dining rooms open across a limestone terrace with broad steps cascading down to a rolling lawn and the beach beyond. Off to one side, a second set of terraces steps down to a cabana, where the tiered pool creates the illusion of fresh water flowing into the sea.

Our Spanish farmhouse is geometrically disciplined, inspired by the Palm Beach, Florida, work of Addison Mizner from the late 1910s and 1920s, as well as by that of George Washington Smith in Montecito, California, from the same period. The detailing is restrained. On the exterior, dark red-tile roofs, terra-cotta cornices, and Tuscan red window frames subtly convey Mediterranean references. Inside, polished mahogany doors set in thick, rough plaster walls, oak-beamed ceilings, and stone floors contribute a sense of permanence and authenticity.

RIGHT
Entrance to garden court.

OVERLEAF
Entrance loggia.

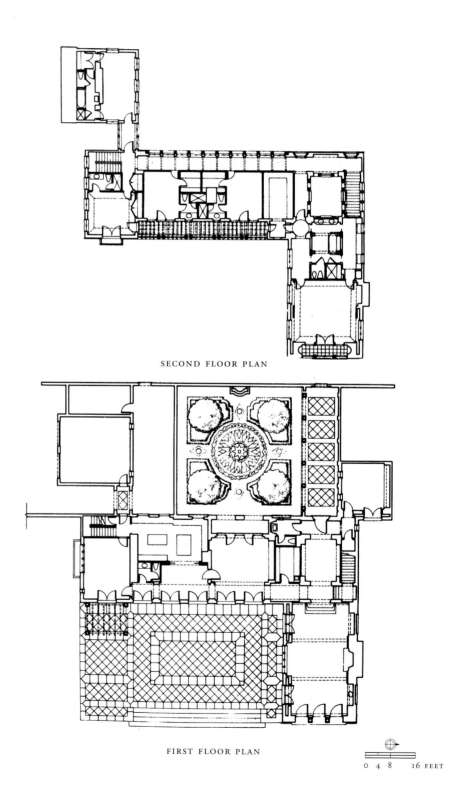

SECOND FLOOR PLAN

FIRST FLOOR PLAN

0   4   8   16 FEET

ROBERT A. M. STERN: HOUSES

LEFT
Pebble garden.

BELOW LEFT
*Dining room looking toward
pebble garden.*

BELOW RIGHT
*Night view of entrance hall
looking toward loggia.*

LEFT

*Connecting hall looking
toward family room.*

BELOW

Living room.

OVERLEAF

East facade.

ROBERT A. M. STERN: HOUSES

LEFT
*Dressing room looking
toward master bedroom.
Master bathroom.*

BELOW
Dressing room detail.

FIRST OVERLEAF
Second-floor hallway.

SECOND OVERLEAF
View from the southeast.

THIRD OVERLEAF
*Twilight view
of sea from pool.*

Entrance (east) facade detail.

ARCHITECT'S COTTAGE

EAST HAMPTON, NEW YORK 1989–1993 Architects design their own houses at great peril, for who wants to be trapped in yesterday's idea? Philip Johnson most famously designed his own Glass House (1949) early on in his career. But he then built its opposite, the brick guest house (1950), about which he soon enough changed his mind, and within two years he drastically remodeled. As his ideas evolved, he would further build on his property, creating an architectural autobiography.

For a long time I resisted building for myself, preferring to tinker with an old house. But in the late 1970s, I acquired a totally nondescript cottage, and in so doing was confronted with the very architectural problem I had long avoided: making a personal statement. I procrastinated, doing nothing until, by chance, I overheard two passersby: "Surely he doesn't live *there*," they exclaimed. In a doomed effort to buy a little more time and avoid the problem, I immediately took my name off the driveway entrance and replaced it with a number. But this was a stopgap measure. Faced with the knowledge that I could procrastinate no longer, I soon enough set out to redesign my comfortably banal cottage into a proper architect's house.

As a consequence of the decision to rebuild, I am the proud owner of what is surely the grandest house in the neighborhood and therefore a fiscal folly. But I enjoy living in my shingled cottage, the design of which has been sifted through the sensibility of Karl Friedrich Schinkel. Schinkel's work in Potsdam, Germany, from the 1820s through the 1840s gave me the idea for the tower that encloses a small bedroom of nearly cubic proportions, and for the diminutive pergola-shaded terrace. These look out to a square of hedgebound lawn, which by happy accident is anchored at each corner by mature oak trees that are almost identical.

Inside, a mock-paneled living room—really a living hall of the sort common in Shingle Style houses of the 1880s—opens through wide French doors to a screened porch, for me the sine qua non of summer life. My bedroom-library, inspired as much by Thomas Jefferson and Sir John Soane as by Schinkel, is the perfect retreat, lined with very, very dark green book cabinets that yield a sense of dense enclosure—permanence, even—and thus provide a very nice contrast to the ephemeral nature of a seaside weekend.

RIGHT
View from the southeast.

FIRST OVERLEAF
Entrance facade.

SECOND OVERLEAF
West facade.

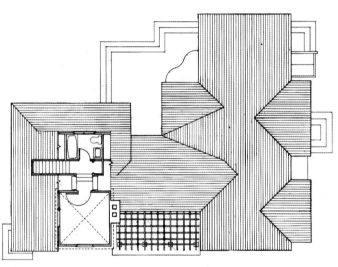

TOWER AND ROOF PLAN

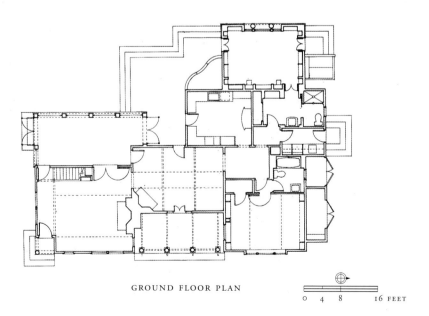

GROUND FLOOR PLAN

0   4   8   16 FEET

ROBERT A. M. STERN: HOUSES

LEFT
Entrance.
Entrance facade detail.

BELOW
West facade detail.

FIRST OVERLEAF
Southeast corner before
construction of tower.

SECOND OVERLEAF
Screened porch.

ROBERT A. M. STERN: HOUSES

LEFT TOP
Living room.

LEFT BOTTOM
Living room.

BELOW
Dining room.

BELOW LEFT
Living room fireplace detail.

BELOW RIGHT
Stairway detail.

RIGHT
Kitchen cabinet.

ROBERT A. M. STERN: HOUSES

LEFT

Master bathroom.

BELOW

Master bedroom.

OVERLEAF

Master bedroom.

RESIDENCE
AT SKIMHAMPTON

EAST HAMPTON, NEW YORK 1992–1993 I think it's safe to say that the clients of this house, long-time friends who were inspired by the success of my own transformed cottage, dreamed of a similar makeover for their 1970s bland Modernist box. But that was not to be, and for good reason. Paul Goldberger described his house as a "rotten little Modern box" of a summer house that he and his wife, Susan Solomon, had purchased seven years before. There were neither the funds nor, after a brief failed attempt, any real inclination to transform the house into an expanded shingled cottage. A shingled wing in our characteristic style would look silly if added on to the Modernist matched-board box.

Given my belief in context, something else was called for, and I really welcomed the challenge to do the "right" thing with the kind of house I had long castigated as decidedly "wrong." Consequently I did what I almost always do—that is, be contextual, even if it meant going Modern. As a result, this is my first Modernist-inspired house in twenty years.

A new wing was set at right angles to the rear of the original house and a screened porch was attached to the front; together the additions yield not only a proper entrance court but also a new facade scaled to the lovely garden that Susan coaxed out of the once scraggly landscape of second-growth oak.

Though the expanded house is Modernist in form, it has behind it twenty years of experience with traditional houses. The revised plan incorporates clearly defined rooms opening off of the new double-height entry. The key openings and the screened porch are framed in a carefully articulated wooden grid and collaborate with the shadow-making pergolas to lift the design beyond the blandly literal vocabulary of walls and windows that had cast such a pall over the original house.

RIGHT
View of entrance hall from stairway.

FIRST OVERLEAF
East facade.

SECOND OVERLEAF
West facade.

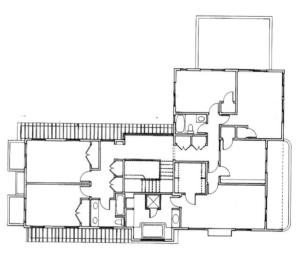

SECOND FLOOR PLAN

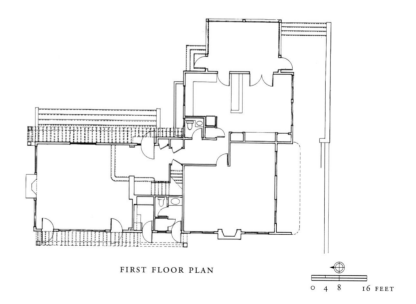

FIRST FLOOR PLAN

0   4   8   16 FEET

ROBERT A. M. STERN: HOUSES

LEFT

Screened porch.

BELOW TOP

Living room.

BELOW BOTTOM

Living room.

RESIDENCE AT CALF CREEK

WATER MILL, NEW YORK 1984–1987 A great achievement of the Shingle Style was the marriage of traditional details and forms with loose-fit, rambling plans in which rooms opened up to each other and to shaded porches. The parallel development of mass and detail distinguished the Shingle Style house on the landscape; it stretched long and low and, where size permitted, seemed as if to float. With its subsumed porches and continuous sheltering roofs punctuated by dormers and anchored by towers, this style, more than any other house type I know, is distinctly American. As such, the genre inspires our work over and over again.

Facing west across Calf Creek, a narrow tributary of Mecox Bay, on the best land of a former farm, the gambrel-roofed house is approached across a tree-lined drive that crosses an open meadow and terminates in a motor court. In compensation for the flat, featureless site, the house itself is deliberately picturesque, combining towers and bays, subsumed porches, and *tholos*-inspired gazebos. Such familiar vernacular elements as dormer windows and projecting bays are counterpointed with more formal Classical elements, including a stylobate, Tuscan columns, and full entablatures. Synthesizing elements of high and low architecture into a complex unity, the overall composition is rooted in local culture yet part of a long-standing and ongoing tradition.

RIGHT
East facade detail.

FIRST OVERLEAF
Approach to house.

SECOND OVERLEAF
South facade.

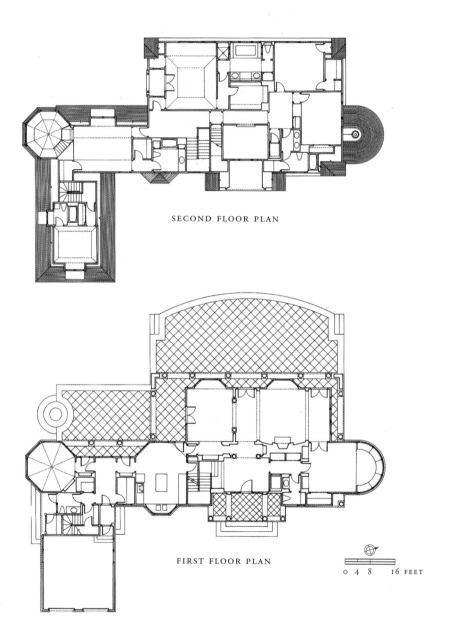

SECOND FLOOR PLAN

FIRST FLOOR PLAN

0 4 8   16 FEET

LEFT

Stair hall.

BELOW

FIRST ROW

*View of living room from
dining room.
Living room.*

SECOND ROW

*Stair hall looking
toward living room.
View of living room
from dining room.*

LEFT
Twilight view of entrance.

BELOW TOP
View from the northeast.

BELOW BOTTOM
View from the south.

FIRST OVERLEAF
Twilight view from the west.

SECOND OVERLEAF
Gazebo.

LEFT
*View from top of tower
to the east.*

RESIDENCE AT WILDERNESS POINT

FISHERS ISLAND, NEW YORK 1986–1989 In many ways this is our quintessential Shingle Style design: capturing water views on three sides and permitting sea breezes to flow freely through the rooms, the one-room-deep house forms a long central mass to which pavilions and such elements as a tower and gazebo have been added in order to form an asymmetrical and picturesque composition.

Great care was exercised in the details.
Windows are not only multipaned,
but some are leaded or have patterned
divisions of glass. Areas of shingles
are also patterned in their coursings.
The stonework anchors house to
site, especially when viewed from the
rocky beach.

Precisely formed individual rooms
open to each other, with the
front hall, living room, and dining
room forming a continuous suite. A
cross axis consisting of a solarium,
breakfast area, and kitchen comprises
a second, informal suite of rooms
and separates the family quarters from
the angled wing of the house, which
incorporates service areas and staff
bedrooms. At the north end of the
second floor, expressed by the large
exterior gambrel, is the master suite
with a small private study above.
The remainder of the second floor is
given over to guest and children's
rooms, one of them an octagonal
space in the tower. Above this
tower room sits an open belvedere
that generously offers views to
Connecticut, Block Island, and even
distant Montauk Point.

RIGHT
Veranda.

OVERLEAF
View from the southwest.

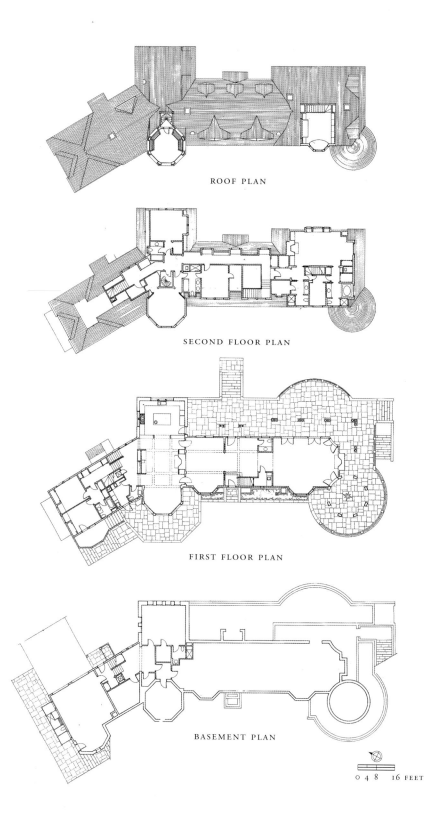

ROOF PLAN

SECOND FLOOR PLAN

FIRST FLOOR PLAN

BASEMENT PLAN

0 4 8   16 FEET

LEFT
Entrance.

BELOW TOP
Entrance (east) facade.

BELOW CENTER
View from the northeast.

BELOW BOTTOM
Approach to house.

LEFT
View along west facade.

BELOW
Tower.

OVERLEAF
Gazebo porch.

ROBERT A. M. STERN: HOUSES

LEFT
Veranda.

BELOW
*View from tower
to the northwest.*

OVERLEAF
Entrance.

ROBERT A. M. STERN: HOUSES

LEFT

Master bathroom detail.

BELOW

Master bedroom detail.

OVERLEAF

View from the west.

RESIDENCE AT POTTERS-VILLE

BEDMINSTER TOWNSHIP, NEW JERSEY 1985–1989

The first of our shingled houses to be built in rolling country rather than by the sea, this house nestles into the brow of a low ridge that crowns a meadow. Approached across a broad pasture on the north side, where the site falls off to reveal a rubble-clad basement story, the house presents a long, low silhouette to the garden on the south. The boldly massed composition comprises elemental forms—two juxtaposed gambrel-roofed volumes pinned by an octagonal stair tower, echoing neighboring barns and silos.

On closer inspection, the farm images give way to the house's main entrance, on the west; or to the short facade, where a pedimented porch lends a note of formality appropriate to rooms devoted to entertaining. Beginning the sequence is the front hall, which doubles as a stage for musical concerts sponsored by the family; the audience for such events sits in the large living room. Living, dining, and family rooms all look past pergola columns to an intimate sunken garden. Reserved for informal daily life is the east end of the house, where a family room opens onto a pedimented screened porch, echoing the entrance but thrust forward to overlook the swimming pool and a broad expanse of meadow.

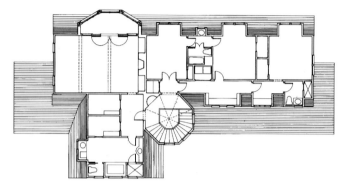

SECOND FLOOR PLAN

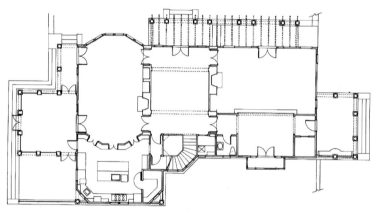

FIRST FLOOR PLAN

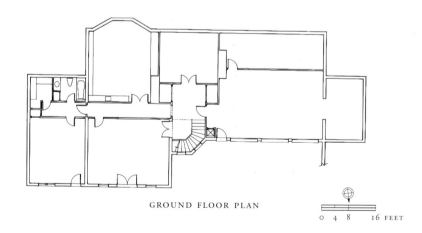

GROUND FLOOR PLAN

0   4   8   16 FEET

LEFT

View from the northwest.

BELOW TOP

View from the southwest.

BELOW CENTER

View from the south.

BELOW BOTTOM

View from the northeast.

OVERLEAF

South facade.

ROBERT A. M. STERN: HOUSES

LEFT

*View of family room
from kitchen.*

BELOW TOP

Family room.

BELOW BOTTOM

Family room.

LEFT

Living room.

BELOW TOP

Living room.

BELOW BOTTOM

Master bedroom.

ROBERT A. M. STERN: HOUSES

RESIDENCE
IN THE MIDWESTERN
UNITED STATES

1990–1993 Bordered by ponds, roadside meadows, and low-rising hills, this beautiful site forced us to abandon our typical strategy of using the house as a wall between the public realm of arrival and the private realm of arcadian garden. Here the long drive swells past an existing barn (later converted into a playhouse) and loops behind the house to the entrance. Landscaping obscures much of the house and its expansive meadow from view during the approach so that visitors do not get a full sense of the place until they pass through the entry vestibule and the living hall to arrive at the Doric porch colonnade that frames the parklike scene.

The house itself—a long, low, rambling mass with shingled walls, flared roofs, and broadly overhanging porches—marries the Shingle Style to the local Greek Revival–inspired farmhouse vernacular. The general informality of the exterior gives way inside to a somewhat grander scale; a double-height, oak-paneled, barrel-vaulted living hall serves as the principal gathering place. Circulation continues along the book-lined gallery, which leads past the dining room to a combined kitchen and family room. This pathway forms a gently skewed axis, a device adopted to help insure privacy for the library and for the ground-floor master bedroom suite.

RIGHT TOP
Entrance (north) facade.

RIGHT BOTTOM
View from the northwest.

OVERLEAF
South facade.

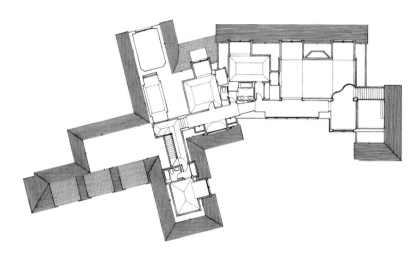

SECOND FLOOR PLAN

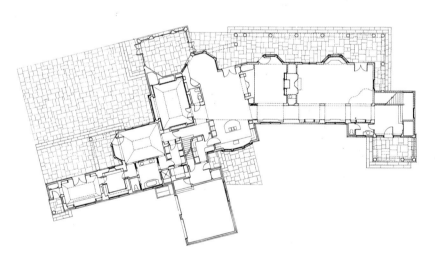

FIRST FLOOR PLAN

0 4 8   16 FEET

LEFT TOP
*View of entry porch
from the west.*

LEFT BOTTOM
View of patio from the south.

BELOW
Screened porch.

BELOW
Gallery.

RIGHT
Stairway and gallery.

OVERLEAF
Family room.

LEFT
*View of living room
from balcony.*

BELOW
Living room.

BELOW TOP
Library.

BELOW BOTTOM
Dining room.

RIGHT
Family room.

ROBERT A. M. STERN: HOUSES

LEFT TOP
Master bedroom.

LEFT BOTTOM
Guest bedroom.

BELOW
Master bathroom.

OVERLEAF
*View from porch
to the southwest.*

SPRUCE LODGE

ROCKY MOUNTAINS 1987–1991 In all respects but its expression, Spruce Lodge is a representative Shingle Style house. But it is that key issue—expression—that makes this house very special within the body of our work. One of our most consistent and controlled houses, with every aspect from landscape to architecture to interior decorating conforming to a single theme, Spruce Lodge exemplifies the nearly mythic American West rather than the American Colonial past. If it has any specific source, Spruce Lodge grows out of the sprawling lodges of the late-nineteenth-century Adirondack camps, where picturesquely massed, log-framed volumes were carefully situated to take advantage of spectacular views.

The plan of Spruce Lodge is free yet precisely articulated, describing an interior landscape of rooms opening easily to each other as well as opening out to porches and balconies. Framed with heavy-timber trusses, the double-height living room is one of our most memorable interior spaces. Close study of Adirondack camps led us to juxtapose geometries of bays and balconies and to incorporate rich, tactile surfaces, including local stone, exposed timber, and elaborately shaped wood shingles.

While Spruce Lodge is a log house, it is not the cabin archetype Abraham Lincoln knew. Differences lie not only in size but also in the very way we used logs to create unique spaces. Our logs were not stacked in the traditional way; our plan is not right-angled, but inflected and bent in response to the peculiarities of the site and to particular views. The twists give the exposed logs a highly dramatic role in the composition. As a result, Spruce Lodge takes on a craggy naturalism that works with its setting.

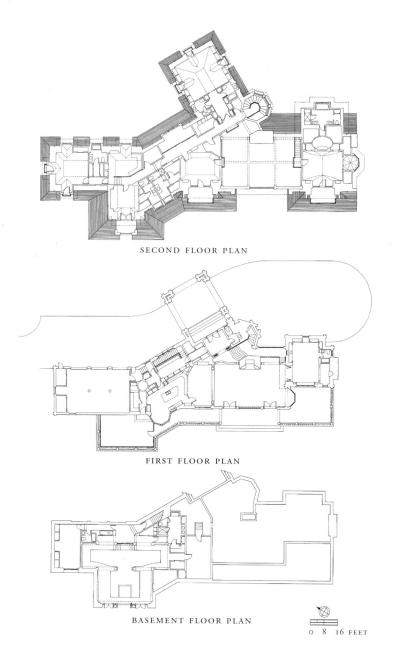

SECOND FLOOR PLAN

FIRST FLOOR PLAN

BASEMENT FLOOR PLAN

0   8   16 FEET

ROBERT A. M. STERN: HOUSES

LEFT TOP
Entrance court.

LEFT BOTTOM
Northeast facade detail.

BELOW TOP
Southwest facade detail.

BELOW BOTTOM
Southwest facade detail.

OVERLEAF
*View of porte cochere
from the east.*

LEFT
*View of main stairway
from dining room.*

BELOW
*View of dining room
from main stairway.*

BELOW
*View of living room
from main entrance.*

RIGHT
*Twilight view of living
and dining rooms from
master bedroom balcony.*

OVERLEAF
*View of living room
with stairway to master
bedroom at rear.*

LEFT
Living room.

BELOW TOP
Stairway tower.

BELOW BOTTOM
Ski hall.

LEFT
Bridge detail.

BELOW LEFT
Bridge detail.

BELOW RIGHT
Bridge detail.

ROBERT A. M. STERN: HOUSES

LEFT
Bridge.

BELOW
Barn detail.

OVERLEAF
Southwest facade.

SKY-VIEW

ASPEN, COLORADO 1987–1990 When asked by the client for whom we had previously designed both the Greenwich Poolhouse and Points of View to design a ski house on Red Mountain in Aspen, Colorado, I was confronted not only by a site totally different from any I had worked with before but also by the fact that there is no singular architectural vernacular in the American West. Many things seem appropriate, including bracketed Victorian cottages, sod or log houses of Scandinavian lineage, houses derived in part from the luxurious camps of the Adirondacks, and ranch houses that have their basis in Spanish colonial haciendas. But none of these seemed quite right for this project.

Skyview is set as high on Red
Mountain as people can build, and
commands a sweeping panorama
across the valley of the town to the ski
slopes on Aspen Mountain. To
reduce the impact on the land, Skyview
was designed in the spirit of a mountain village, with a central gabled main
block and subsidiary interconnected
volumes gathered around it, all united
by the strong geometry of metal-clad
vaulted roofs. Waggish neighbors refer
to the composition as that of a main
house and a "wagon train" pulled up
to it, so I must have touched some very
basic chord of local culture, though
the local and specific meaning of the
design is not anecdotal.

Colorado sandstone and tawny stucco
pick up the colors of the landscape,
metal roofs speak of the casual closure
of typical Western buildings, and heavy
wood framing lends a tectonic discipline to the whole. Skyview is entered
from above, where a wood truss forms
a pediment carried on primitive Doric
columns. A dramatic flight of stairs,
paneled in wood to suggest rustication,
extends the village metaphor—it's like
a stepped street in a hill town, with
wood-framed portals leading to various
houses that in reality are self-contained
suites of rooms. At the bottom, in
keeping with the hill-town metaphor,
the living and dining rooms, as well as
the balcony and terraces, come together
to suggest a piazza.

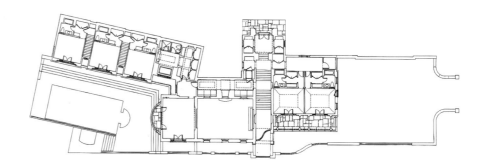

SECOND FLOOR PLAN

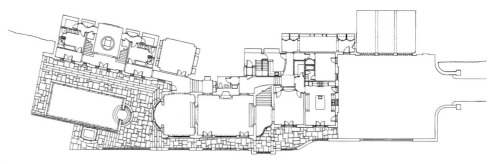

FIRST FLOOR PLAN

0 4 8   16 FEET

ROBERT A. M. STERN: HOUSES

LEFT

FIRST ROW
South facade detail.
East facade detail.

SECOND ROW
Entrance.
*View of east facade
showing dining room
terrace (below) and guest
room balcony (above).*

BELOW
Roof detail.

OVERLEAF
*View of pool terrace with
children's wing on the left.*

BELOW
*View from guest room
balcony to the southwest.*

RIGHT
View from the south.

LEFT
Stair hall.

BELOW LEFT
*View of stair hall
from exterior.*

BELOW RIGHT
Handrail detail.

BELOW
*View of living room
from stairway landing.*

RIGHT
Living room detail.

OVERLEAF
*Night view of pool
terrace and children's wing.*

THE GABLES

WOODLYNNE, BINGHAM FARMS, MICHIGAN 1987–1991

The second house built at Woodlynne, the Gables, was designed in close consultation with the couple who had commissioned the house. Though the site was somewhat constrained, it enjoyed borrowed views so that the house could be placed well back from the road. Planned in connection with the house were extensive gardens with a distinctly English character that is very much in keeping with local tradition, seen at its best in Albert Kahn's Cranbrook House (1907) in the neighboring village of Bloomfield Hills.

RIGHT
View through garden gate.

OVERLEAF
View from the north.

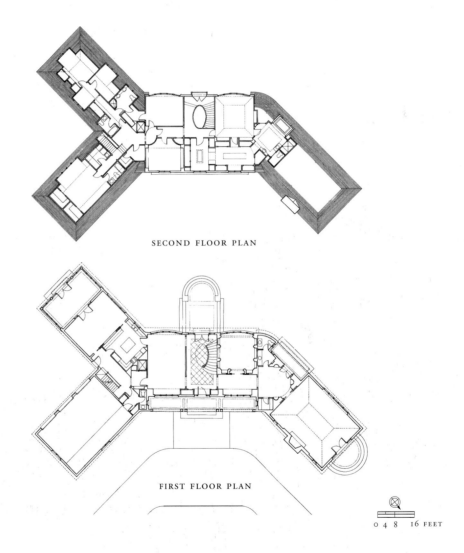

SECOND FLOOR PLAN

FIRST FLOOR PLAN

0 4 8   16 FEET

LEFT
*View from garden
to the north.*

BELOW
View from the west.

BELOW TOP
Family room.

BELOW BOTTOM
Living room.

RIGHT
Stair hall in guest house.

RESIDENCE AT APAQUOGUE

EAST HAMPTON, NEW YORK 1989–1993 The most Classical of our shingled houses, the Residence at Apaquogue looks for inspiration to the same late-eighteenth- and early-nineteenth-century East Hampton residences that inspired the first resort builders one hundred years ago. These earlier architects preferred the formality of the Georgian aesthetic to the more naturalistic seventeenth-century farmhouses. Though it looks unlike our other work on the south shore, it is nonetheless very much of the place. Thus a tradition is honored and continued but in a different way.

This is a fairly large house, but a fictive history was created to justify an agglomerative composition that helps to establish a sense of intimacy. For example, the north wing, containing the family room and garage, appears to be an earlier saltbox structure to which the grander, symmetrical house was later added. Such a situation was not unusual one hundred years ago and can be seen to great effect at Stanford White's Breese House in nearby Southampton (1907), where it looks as if a palatial version of Mount Vernon were added onto an existing farmhouse. At the south end of our house, a library and screened porch also appear to be typical later additions. The Apaquogue house is much smaller and simpler than White's design, yet it too gains vivacity from the bold contrast between large and small scale: giant order pilasters flank the central entrance facade and support a deep-bracketed eave; slender, paired colonettes support the entry porch.

Inside, the large rooms open onto one another through wide double doorways so that there is an easy flow between them. Although the basic mass and the details are traditional, the clarity of the plan, the simple proportions of the rooms, and the large scale of the light-flooding windows make this very much a house of our time.

RIGHT
View from the southeast.

FIRST OVERLEAF
Entrance (east) facade detail.

SECOND OVERLEAF
South facade.

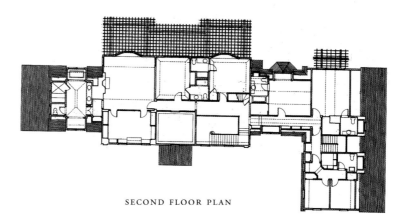

SECOND FLOOR PLAN

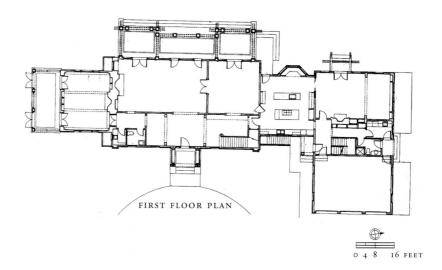

FIRST FLOOR PLAN

0 4 8   16 FEET

LEFT
Entrance hall.

BELOW
*View of living room
from entrance hall.*

FIRST OVERLEAF
*Entrance hall looking
toward library.*

SECOND OVERLEAF
*View from living room
into dining room.*

ROBERT A. M. STERN: HOUSES

PROJECT CREDITS

WESTCHESTER COUNTY RESIDENCE
Westchester County, New York
1974–1976
Architects-in-Charge: Daniel L. Colbert,
Jeremy P. Lang
Assistants: Robert S. Buford, Joan Chan,
Ronne Fisher

GREENWICH POOLHOUSE
Greenwich, Connecticut
1973–1974
Architect-in-Charge: Daniel L. Colbert
Assistants: Joan Chan, Ronne Fisher,
William Schweber, Clifford M.
Thatcher-Renshaw

NEW YORK CITY TOWNHOUSE
New York, New York
1974–1975
Architect-in-Charge: Jeremy P. Lang
Assistants: Wayne Berg, Ronne Fisher,
Laurence Marner

LLEWELLYN PARK RESIDENCE
Llewellyn Park, New Jersey
1979–1981
Architect-in-Charge: Anthony Cohn
Assistants: Ethelind Coblin, Alan Gerber,
Gavin Macrae-Gibson

POINTS OF VIEW
Mount Desert Island, Maine
PHASE I 1975–1976
Architect-in-Charge: Daniel L. Colbert
PHASE II 1992–1993
Architect-in-Charge: Armand LeGardeur
Assistants: Elizabeth Kozarec, Lee Ledbetter

RESIDENCE AT CHILMARK
Martha's Vineyard, Massachusetts
1979–1983
Architect-in-Charge: Roger Seifter
Assistant: John Krieble
Interior Design Associate: Alan Gerber

RESIDENCE AT FARM NECK
Martha's Vineyard, Massachusetts
1980–1983
Architect-in-Charge: Roger Seifter
Assistant: John Krieble
Interior Design Associate: Ronne Fisher

TREADWAY HOUSE
Southampton, New York
1983–1985
Architect-in-Charge: Randy Correll
Assistants: Joseph W. Dick, David Eastman

RESIDENCE AT HARDSCRABBLE
East Hampton, New York
1983–1985
Architect-in-Charge: Armand LeGardeur
Assistants: Kerry Moran, Kaarin Taipale
Landscape Associate: Robert Ermerins
Interior Design Associate: Ronne Fisher

LAWSON HOUSE
East Quogue, New York
1979–1981
Architect-in-Charge: John Averitt
Assistants: Terry Brown, John Krieble,
Charles D. Warren

RESIDENCE ON RUSSIAN HILL
San Francisco, California
1985–1989
Architect-in-Charge: Alan Gerber
Project Associates: Kristin McMahon,
Elizabeth Thompson
Assistant: Ken McIntyre-Horito
Associated Architect: Richard Hannum

EAST HAMPTON RESIDENCE
East Hampton, New York
1980–1983
Architect-in-Charge: Roger Seifter
Assistant: Terry Brown
Interior Design Associate: Ronne Fisher

MARBLEHEAD RESIDENCE
Marblehead, Massachusetts
1984–1987
Architect-in-Charge: Roger Seifter
Assistants: Caroline Hancock, Kaarin Taipale

SUNSTONE
Quogue, New York
1984–1987
Architect-in-Charge: Randy Correll
Assistants: Thomas Nohr, Constance Treadwell

RED OAKS
Cohasset, Massachusetts
1992–1995
Architect-in-Charge: Randy Correll
Assistant: Elizabeth Kozarec
Landscape Associate: Robert Ermerins

MILL NECK RESIDENCE
Mill Neck, New York
1981–1983
Architect-in-Charge: Charles D. Warren
Assistants: Alan Gerber, John Ike
Interior Design Assistant: Alan Gerber

HEWLETT HARBOR RESIDENCE
Hewlett Harbor, New York
1984–1988
Architect-in-Charge: Charles D. Warren
Assistants: Re Hagele, Armand LeGardeur,
Grant Marani, Jenny Peng, Elizabeth Thompson
Interior Design Associate: Lisa Maurer
Landscape Associate: Robert Ermerins

RESIDENCE IN STARWOOD
Aspen, Colorado
1991–1996
Architect-in-Charge: Armand LeGardeur
Project Associate: Augusta Barone
Assistants: Adam Anuszkiewicz,
Victoria Delgado, Luis Rueda-Salazar
Landscape Associate: Brian Sawyer
Interior Design Associate: Raúl Morillas
Interior Design Assistant: Chris Powell

DEAL RESIDENCE
Deal, New Jersey
1982–1984
Architect-in-Charge: John Ike
Assistant: Thomas A. Kligerman
Interior Design Associate: Ronne Fisher

VILLA IN NEW JERSEY
Deal, New Jersey
1983–1989
Architect-in-Charge: Thomas A. Kligerman
Senior Assistants: William T. Georgis,
Arthur Chabon
Assistants: Augusta Barone, Victoria Casasco,
Berndt Dams, Natalie Jacobs, Laurie Kerr,
Françoise Sogno
Landscape Associate: Robert Ermerins
Interior Design Assistants: Ingrid Armstrong,
Stephan Johnson, Tanya Kelly, Lisa Maurer

RESIDENCE AT RIVER OAKS
Houston, Texas
1988–1992
Architect-in-Charge: Roger Seifter
Senior Assistant: John Berson
Assistants: Abigail Huffman,
Kristin McMahon, Daniel Romauldez
Associate Architect: Richard Fitzgerald
and Associates
Landscape Associate: Robert Ermerins
Landscape Assistant: Laura Schoenbaum
Interior Design Associate: Raúl Morillas
Interior Design Assistants: Paul McDonnell,
Alice Yiu

ELBERON RESIDENCE
Elberon, New Jersey
1985–1989
Architect-in-Charge: John Ike
Project Associate: Augusta Barone
Assistants: Charles Barrett,
Grant Marani, Pat Tiné
Landscape Associate: Robert Ermerins
Landscape Assistant: Stephanie Abrams
Interior Design Associate: Lisa Maurer
Interior Design Assistant: Alice Yiu

ARCHITECT'S COTTAGE
East Hampton, New York
1979; 1989–1993
Architect-in-Charge: Randy Correll
Assistant: William C. Skelsey
Landscape Associate: Robert Ermerins
Landscape Assistant: Charlotte Frieze
Interior Design Associate: Raúl Morillas
Interior Design Assistant: Patricia Burns

RESIDENCE AT SKIMHAMPTON
East Hampton, New York
1992–1993
Architect-in-Charge: Randy Correll
Senior Assistant: Daniel Romauldez

RESIDENCE AT CALF CREEK
Water Mill, New York
1984–1987
Architect-in-Charge: Armand LeGardeur
Senior Assistant: Luis Rueda-Salazar
Landscape Associate: Robert Ermerins
Interior Design Associate: Lisa Maurer

RESIDENCE AT WILDERNESS POINT
Fishers Island, New York
1986–1989
Architect-in-Charge: Randy Correll
Assistants: Yvonne Galindo, James Joseph
Landscape Associate: Robert Ermerins
Landscape Assistants: Stephanie Abrams,
William C. Skelsey

RESIDENCE AT POTTERSVILLE
Bedminster Township, New Jersey
1985–1989
Architect-in-Charge: Randy Correll
Assistants: Deirdre O'Farrelly, Olivia Rowan
Interior Design Associate: Randy Correll

RESIDENCE IN THE MIDWESTERN
UNITED STATES
1990–1993
Architect-in-Charge: Roger Seifter
Project Associate: John Berson
Senior Assistant: Diane Smith
Assistants: Gary Brewer, Randy Correll,
Abigail Huffman, Daniel Romauldez,
Elizabeth Valella, Rosamund Young
Landscape Associate: Robert Ermerins
Landscape Assistant: Charlotte Frieze
Interior Design Associate: Raúl Morillas
Interior Design Assistants: Paul McDonnell,
Witten Singer

SPRUCE LODGE
Rocky Mountains
1987–1991
Architect-in-Charge, Design and Construction
Documents: Thomas A. Kligerman
Architect-in-Charge, Construction:
Arthur Chabon
Assistants: Silvina Goefron, Timothy Haines,
Abigail Huffman, Valerie Hughes, Robert Miller,
Warren Van Wees
Landscape Associate: Robert Ermerins
Landscape Assistant: William C. Skelsey
Interior Design Associate: Raúl Morillas
Interior Design Assistants: Nancy Boszhardt,
Deborah Emery, Stephan Johnson

SKYVIEW
Aspen, Colorado
1987–1990
Architect-in-Charge: Armand LeGardeur
Assistants: Karen Small, Derrick Smith
Landscape Associate: Robert Ermerins
Landscape Assistant: William C. Skelsey

THE GABLES
Woodlynne, Bingham Farms, Michigan
1987–1991
Architect-in-Charge: Grant Marani
Senior Assistant: Jay A. Waronker
Assistants: Joseph Andriola, W. David
Henderson, Lee Ledbetter, Rosamund Young
Interior Design Associate: Raúl Morillas
Senior Interior Design Assistant:
Paul McDonnell
Interior Design Assistants: Deborah Emery,
Stephan Johnson, Leslie Radziemski, Alice Yiu

RESIDENCE AT APAQUOGUE
East Hampton, New York
1989–1993
Architect-in-Charge: Randy Correll
Senior Assistant: Daniel Romauldez
Assistant: Gary Brewer
Landscape Associate: Robert Ermerins
Landscape Assistant: Charlotte Frieze

ILLUSTRATION CREDITS